Clicker Fun

Dog Tricks and Games Using Positive Reinforcement

by Deborah Jones, Ph.D.

HOWLN MOON PRESS

CLICKER FUN

Dog Tricks and Games Using Positive Reinforcement

by Deborah Jones, Ph.D.

Illustrated by Susan L. Coons

Published by HOWLN MOON PRESS
203 State Road, P.O. Box 238, Eliot, ME 03903

Library of Congress Cataloging in Publication Data

Jones, Deborah (Deborah Ann)
Clicker fun : dog tricks and games using positive reinforcement / by Deborah Jones.
p. cm.
ISBN 1-888994-08-8 (alk. paper)
1. Dogs - - Training.   2. Games for dogs.   3. Reinforcement (Psychology)
I. Title.

SF431.J66 1998
636.7'0887 - - dc21

98-9796
CIP

Table of Contents

ACKNOWLEDGMENTS

There are so many people I'd like thank for their help, support, and inspiration. First, I'd like to thank my family for their understanding of my hobby turned profession. No matter how odd they find it that I prefer dog training to human psychology, they keep it to themselves.

I'd like to thank my business partner, Liz Mancz, for her moral support and superb proofreading and editing abilities. A huge thanks also to my friends and instructors at Planet Canine (Karen Ricker, Sharon Darmstadt, Vilma Kistner, Kathy Darmstadt) for making my job so much easier and more enjoyable.

The people who contribute to the internet discussion lists have been a wonderful source of creative ideas. Thanks to all the members of clicktrain, click-l, and the APDT discussion lists. Thank you to all the members of the Association of Pet Dog Trainers as well. Your generous sharing of ideas and information has been inspirational.

Thank you to those who helped give this book the right "look". In particular, I appreciate all the work of Gary Miller, the very patient photographer, and Susan Coons, the very talented illustrator. Also, thanks to the following people and dogs for their participation in the photo shoot: Karen Ricker with Shiva (Mini-Dachshund) and Tarra (Coonhound), Vilma Kistner with Java (Bernese Mountain Dog) and Buddy (Pembroke Welsh Corgi), and Liz Mancz with Rin (Rough Collie) and Jessie (Smooth Collie).

My best teachers have been all of the dogs and owners I have come in contact with over the years. Many of the most challenging have been the most educational and I appreciate all the lessons I've learned.

Finally, of course, thanks to my two best canine friends, Katie and Sully. You've both enriched my life in so many ways. You've taught me much more than I could ever teach you. I treasure every day we have together.

ABOUT THE AUTHOR & HER DOGS

I am a psychologist with a Ph.D. in social psychology. I started my academic career as an undergraduate working in a rat lab, training rats to press levers, run mazes, climb ladders, etc. I learned the ins and outs of learning theory and operant conditioning. In graduate school I focused on studying human social interactions.

It was also in graduate school that Katie, my black Lab, came into my life. Katie was an eighteen-month-old rescue dog who had been in two homes. For the six months before I got her she had basically lived as a feral dog, running loose in the woods. I'd owned dogs my whole life, but never one like Katie. She was sweet and smart, but also independent and tough. I quickly found that traditional, force-based training methods would not work with her. She absolutely refused to work if it wasn't enjoyable. That's when I decided to apply operant conditioning as I'd learned it in school. The results were amazing! She learned cute tricks, she learned basic behavior, she became certified as a Therapy Dog, she even learned AKC obedience exercises.

While training Katie I started instructing at a local AKC obedience club. We added a tricks class, and started incorporated some 'clicker' training into the curriculum with good results. I learned that other people had already discovered that operant conditioning methods were perfect for dog training. So I read everything I could find, attended seminars when I could, watched videos, and connected to clicker lists on the internet.

Then I met Sully. Sully was a twelve-week-old Golden Retriever. His owner called me for a behavior consultation because he was 'aggressive'. What I found was a highly energetic, overreactive, absolutely goofy, yet very intelligent golden ball of fur. His owners wanted a couch potato dog. So Sully came home with me and became my completely clicker trained boy. It hasn't always been an easy road with Sully. There's been lots of experimentation. I made mistakes along the way. However, he still has an absolute love of training, which was always my number one goal for him.

When Sully was young I moved to take a teaching job at a large university. I joined another AKC obedience club and started instructing for them. With time, I was asked to become Training Director. I instituted clicker classes and tricks and games classes into the schedule. The students loved them!

After I started my own training school, I continued to experiment with training methods and with class material. What I've learned over time is that behavior is behavior. Teaching a straight sit is no different than teaching a high five. If you approach all training with a fun attitude, your dog will enjoy the process as well. I've worked with thousands of dogs and students in group and private classes, as well as in consultations for behavior problems. In my experiences, I've seen the amazing results that can be obtained using training methods based on operant conditioning principles. These methods are fair, humane, and enjoyable. I can't imagine training any other way.

PREFACE: WHY I TEACH TRICKS & GAMES

I love spending time with my dogs. Whether we're obedience training, taking walks, playing fetch, or just spending quiet time together, I enjoy being with them. Something I've noticed over the years is how they love to play and explore. They seem to be curious about new things and to love different and unusual activities. Teaching them tricks and games seemed a natural extension of our relationship.

Teaching tricks and games is a great way to get to know your dog better. How to motivate your dog, how fast your dog picks up on new ideas, how much repetition she can stand, and how long it takes to get a finished product can all be learned in trick training. Besides, it's fun, easy, and there's no pressure to be perfect.

Once you learn how to train your dog to do tricks, you can train nearly any behavior. If you think about it, even obedience exercises are tricks. Behavior is behavior, and training a dog to roll over is no different than training a dog to recall. Usually, the difference is in the trainer's attitude. Many people approach obedience training as serious business. They see tricks as funny and silly. However, there is no difference to the dog. They're simply learning to perform a specific behavior, or series of behaviors, on cue.

Sometimes tricks can turn into very useful behaviors. When I had back problems last year and couldn't bend over, I was able to have my Lab, Katie, pick up and bring me my slippers, phone, newspaper, etc. It was interesting to me to see her reaction to these requests. I would almost swear she was proud of herself!

Because I teach a number of classes in human psychology, as well as dog obedience classes, I find it very helpful to have my dogs demonstrate learning principles and methods by performing tricks. My students are usually very attentive, and they tend to remember information presented this way. Also, Katie is registered through the Delta Society as a therapy dog. We make visits to hospitals and nursing homes. Her tricks, even the simple ones, are always a big hit.

Teaching tricks and games in obedience classes is a great way to make training fun and interesting. Students and their dogs relax, which leads to improved learning for both humans and canines. While most people are happy with a well-behaved pet who is under control, they are usually very pleased with a dog who can perform a cute trick. This dog is more likely to get positive attention from people and to benefit from continued interaction. This dog is less likely to have relationship problems with its owner, and more likely to stay in its home (one of my major goals as a trainer). Please approach this book with the easygoing spirit in which it is offered. Relax, enjoy, play, discover, learn.

1 *Introduction*

CHAPTER 1: AN INTRODUCTION TO OPERANT CONDITIONING & CLICKER TRAINING

INTRODUCTION

Dog training should be fun for the trainer and for the dog. Don't get me wrong, I think it's very important to have a well-behaved pet. However, the learning process can be interesting and enjoyable. It doesn't have to be based on physical domination, fear, or pain.

Most dogs are simple, honest creatures. They seek pleasure and avoid pain. They operate on basic drives and desires (food, water, companionship, sex). They don't have hidden agendas or complex motivations for their behaviors. They do what feels good. An understanding of this aspect of the canine psyche allows us to create an environment in which we control access to the good things that dogs enjoy. This control of the environment allows us to control their behavior. Your dog wants a cookie? He has to sit to get it. Next time cookies are present, he's more likely to sit again. Your dog wants to chase squirrels in the yard? He has to do a down/stay by the door first. Learned behavior is the result of experience. In particular, behavior is ruled by the consequences it produces. A behavior that leads to a pleasant event is likely to be repeated; a behavior that leads to an unpleasant event is not.

Learning can be fun. It's not necessarily a serious endeavor. In particular, when teaching your dog tricks and playing games, it's hard to take yourself too seriously. After all, it's not brain surgery. Nobody dies if you make mistakes. If your dog doesn't grasp the concept of 'high five', it's just not that big of a deal. When learning becomes difficult, both people and dogs try to avoid it. And who can blame them? I'd rather take a walk than do calculus. Many dogs would rather play fetch than practice heeling. I believe that the key is to make the work seem like play. If it's fun, everybody enjoys the process. Plus, you enhance your relationship with your pet and end up with a trained dog. What could be better?

TERMINOLOGY

The basis of the training methods presented in this book is ***operant conditioning*** (OC), a scientifically tested learning theory. OC principles were first discovered and tested by psychologists such as John Watson and B.F. Skinner. At the time that OC principles were first presented, they were considered quite radical. OC suggests that learning is predictable, that it is governed by laws. It also suggests that the underlying process of learning is basically the same for all creatures: cockroaches, pigs, dogs, apes, humans, etc.

There are some very specific terms and definitions that are commonly used in OC and that I will use throughout this book. It's important that you understand these terms and their meanings. If you're already familiar with this information, you can move on.

Operant conditioning (OC). OC is a learning theory that focuses on the consequences as the controlling factors for behavior. The subject 'operates' on the environment, and certain consequences occur. The type of consequence (pleasant or unpleasant) determines how likely it is that the behavior will be repeated. For example, you volunteer for a class demonstration and the teacher embarrasses you. Your future volunteering behavior will probably decrease, at least with that teacher. On the other hand, if you volunteer for a class demonstration and the teacher gives you a dollar, your future volunteering behavior will probably increase. The consequences have influenced your future behavior.

Positive reinforcement (+R). +R involves applying a pleasant consequence after a desired behavior. The purpose of reinforcement is to increase behavior. For example, your dog is lying quietly at your feet. You lean down, pet the dog and say "good dog". Your dog is now more likely to lie quietly at your feet in the future.

Negative reinforcement (-R). This is the one most people get wrong. -R involves removing something unpleasant when a desired behavior occurs. Think of positive as adding something and negative as subtracting something. In negative reinforcement, you remove an ongoing, unpleasant stimulus when the dog performs the desired behavior. The reinforcement comes with the removal of the unpleasant event. Our dogs are actually experts at using negative reinforcement on us. Your dog barks a high-pitched shrill bark to get you to let him outside. To turn off the unpleasant event (barking) you quickly open the door and let him out. The dog reinforces you by stopping the barking. In the future, you're likely to open the door quickly when the barking starts. Door opening behavior has been negatively reinforced.

Positive punishment (+P). +P involves applying an unpleasant stimulus in order to decrease the likelihood of an undesired behavior. The purpose of punishment is to decrease a behavior. If your dog barks and you squirt her with a water pistol, you've applied an unpleasant stimulus (unless you have a retriever!) This is likely to decrease barking in the future.

Negative punishment (-P). -P involves removing a pleasant stimulus in order to decrease behavior. For example, your puppy is nipping at your hands in play. You get up, walk away, and ignore the puppy. You are removing a pleasant stimulus (yourself as a playmate) in an effort to decrease the nipping behavior.

Add • Remove

	Add	Remove
Pleasant	**+R**	**-P**
Unpleasant	**+P**	**-R**

**Note: Positive refers to adding something, negative refers to subtracting something. Reinforcement is meant to increase a behavior, punishment is meant to decrease a behavior. The illustrated grid demonstrates these relationships.

Primary reinforcer (PR). A PR is something that is intrinsically rewarding to the subject. It has internal properties that the subject perceives as pleasant. For most creatures, food is the ultimate PR. For some dogs, playing fetch or chasing a ball might be a PR while others could care less.

Conditioned (secondary) reinforcer (CR). A CR is something that signals the arrival of the PR. A CR and a PR are paired a number of times until the subject responds to the CR in the same way as to the PR. This was Ivan Pavlov's major finding with his slobbering dogs. The dogs began to drool when they heard the food bowls clanging, even before the food was present. Pavlov discovered that they could associate sounds, people, and any number of visual stimuli (lights, etc.) with food and get this response. In humans, the strongest CR available is money. It has been associated with every PR imaginable.

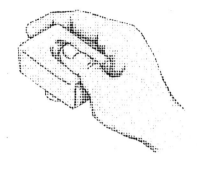

Whenever anything is referred to as conditioned, that means the response has been learned; it is not a naturally-occurring behavior. Primary reinforcers have natural responses. Dogs see food and they drool. No one has to teach them this. Conditioned reinforcers must be learned through association. A clicker can make an excellent CR. There will be a description of a clicker and an explanation of its use in the 'Getting Started' section.

Click and treat (CT). The instruction to CT means to first click, then give your dog a PR. This is always carried out with a click first, followed by a PR. The click needs to become a signal that the PR is on its way. The power of the click is in its association with the PR. You can use any PR that your dog loves. Food is the most common and the easiest to use. However, toys, games, play, praise, and interesting smells are all possible PRs. Again, it depends on your dog's reaction to any of these things. A Coonhound may be much more reinforced by the scent of raccoon than by food. Observe your dog's behavior and let her 'tell' you what she most enjoys, then gain control of it and use it as a PR.

Continuous reinforcement. In the early stages of learning any new behavior, continuous reinforcement is used. This means that every time the behavior is performed, the dog is reinforced. it's important to use continuous reinforcement in this early phase because it is giving important information. By reinforcing you are telling your dog "Bingo! You got that right!" Lack of reinforcement is like saying "Keep trying, you haven't gotten it right yet."

Variable (partial) reinforcement (VR). Once a behavior has been well-learned, you can move from continuous to variable reinforcement. Instead of reinforcing every correct response, you only reinforce some of them. Moving to VR too soon will cause the behavior to degenerate, so you must be sure that the behavior is solid and well-learned. There are a number of different types of VR, the most commonly used type in dog training is variable ratio (reinforcing after a random number of responses). Using this reinforcement schedule keeps the animal guessing about when reinforcement might occur and keeps the response strong.

Extinction. A behavior can be extinguished (disappear) by removing its reinforcement. All behaviors are maintained because they are reinforcing. If you can figure out what the reinforcer is and remove it, you can get rid of the behavior. Whenever you use extinction you can expect to see an 'extinction burst', an increase in the undesirable behavior before it disappears. Extinction bursts are predictable and will go away if ignored.

Fading. Fading is gradually removing the cue or stimulus that prompts the behavior. For example, when first training your dog to respond to a hand signal for 'sit', you would use a large, exaggerated movement. Over time, you can fade the signal by using less and less movement. At some point, you might be able to just use a finger movement for the cue.

THE BASICS

The most important central principle in OC is the following: ***Behavior is governed by its consequences.*** It's not what comes before a behavior that determines its occurrence as much as what comes after. In traditional dog training methods, the signal or command was thought to prompt the behavior. OC has clearly shown that the results of the behavior have much more influence on its probability than do the antecedents. You can break this sequence of events down into 3 parts known as the ABCs of training. A = antecedent (what precedes the behavior), B = behavior, C = consequence (what follows the behavior). I'll expand a bit on each of these components.

Antecedents
Signal, cue, prompt, command. The purpose of any of these antecedents is to elicit (bring out) a behavior. In OC methods, the cue is not introduced until the behavior is already being performed reliably. For example, to teach a dog to sit the dog would be lured into a sit using a food target a number of times until the dog always sat when the food target was presented. Then the verbal cue "sit" would be added just before the lure. After pairing the verbal cue with the lure a number of times, the dog would begin sitting on the verbal cue alone.

Behavior
There are a number of ways to get behaviors to occur. Some dogs continually offer many behaviors throughout the day (think of a Jack Russell Terrier!) Dogs with this type of personality and activity level are ideal for training using OC methods. You'll get lots of chances to reinforce freely offered behaviors. Other dogs are canine couch potatoes and do as little as possible. This could be due to age, physical condition, personality, or prior learning. It takes a bit more effort to get this type of dog to open up, get creative, and try out behaviors.

Many behaviors actually contain a large number of smaller component parts. Instead of teaching the overall behavior, it's easiest to teach each small part separately, then string them together for the finished product. To be an effective trainer it's important to be able to 'break down' a behavior into its simplest parts and teach each part separately.

Shaping. Shaping is one of the most common ways to mold desirable behaviors. You can think of shaping as selectively choosing and reinforcing the types of behaviors that you want and ignoring everything else. Shaping is accomplished in stages, through approximations of the desired behavior. For example, let's say you're trying to teach a puppy to lay down. Instead of waiting for a complete down (elbows and butt on the floor) to occur before reinforcing, you might first reinforce whenever the head is close to the floor, then for a play bow, then for a more complete down. The speed with which you can move through these steps depends on the behaviors the dog offers. Some dogs 'get it' right away. They start trying to figure out what it takes to get reinforced. With others, the process can take a bit longer.

Luring. In many cases you can use luring to elicit reinforceable behaviors. A lure is any object that can retain the dog's focus and attention. Food is an easy lure. You can think of a food lure as a 'nose magnet'. A dog's nose pretty naturally follows it as long as the food is desirable and the dog is motivated to obtain the food. You can increase your chances for successful luring by having a hungry dog and a wonderful food treat. Let's say you wanted to lure the dog to spin instead of waiting for behaviors you could shape. You'd show the dog the lure by putting it right in front of the dog's nose, then move it in a circle around the dog at nose height. The nose should follow the food. If you lure correctly and maintain the dog's interest the dog might give an approximation of a spin.

One problem with luring rather than shaping is that people don't 'fade' the lure over time. The dog waits for the lure and does not attempt to perform the behavior in its absence. Also, luring encourages some dogs to remain passive and wait for direction, rather than to actively try new behaviors. In many cases, a weakened version of the lure can become the signal, and this works well. In other cases, you may want to use a verbal signal or some different cue. This is not a difficult process, but it does require gradually fading the lure while adding the new signal/cue right before the lure. If you start teaching a sit by luring with food, you need to gradually work on removing the food from your hand. You might use the same hand motion that you did when first luring, but keep the food in your pocket. Once the dog is used to this, you might put the food on a table instead of on your person. All of these steps take thought, time, and planning.

Consequences

As I said earlier, consequences are the keys to behavior change. You need to know your dog well to understand which consequences are reinforcing and which are punishing. Close observation of your dog's preferred objects and activities can give you ideas for effective reinforcers. Some dogs will do backflips for a squeaky toy. Others turn up their noses at anything less than filet mignon. Good trainers work hard on making themselves reinforcing for their dogs. Special games played between the dog and owner can be very rewarding for both. In particular, many dogs love chase games (both as the chaser and the chasee!) I recently saw a very creative trainer who was blowing bubbles for her dog to pop as a reinforcer.

By the same reasoning, punishments (when and if used) must be specific to the individual. For some dogs, a stern look is very unpleasant and quite punishing. In my personal opinion, punishment has absolutely no place in trick and game training.

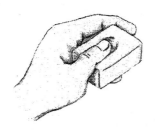

2 *Getting Started*

CHAPTER 2: GETTING STARTED: FUNDAMENTAL EXERCISES & SKILLS

CLICKER CONDITIONING

Clickers started out as children's toys. They were metal shapes, often crickets or other animals, that made a metallic 'click' sound when squeezed. The clickers commonly used by dog trainers today have been redesigned for easier use and more durability. A dog trainer's clicker is a very small rectangular plastic box with a flexible metal interior. Pushing down on one end of the metal makes the clicking sound. At first the sound has no meaning, but after a number of pairings with food, the dog will react to the click in nearly the same way he reacts to food (think Pavlov). A clicker is a very good CR. It makes a unique and unusual sound. Most dogs have never heard anything like it before. This is good because it doesn't have any preexisting associations, either positive or negative.

Many trainers express a desire to use a word as a verbal CR rather than using the clicker. It has been found that a verbal CR is often not clear enough or precise enough. Your dog has been hearing your voice for a long time and often tunes it out (sorry, but this can be true). Also, your voice changes depending on your mood, the time of day, the weather, etc. and doesn't display the consistent quality that a clicker does.

Having said all that, verbal CRs are still useful tools, just not as clear and precise as a clicker. Condition a special word in the same way you condition the clicker. It can be used in situations where a clicker is not available (though clicker trainers seem to stash them everywhere), not acceptable (the obedience ring), or is too unwieldy (your hands are full). The best verbal CRs are only used for that purpose. Pick a word you won't use in everyday interactions or conversations. The way you say the word (pitch and tone) is very important as well.

This initial stage of clicker training is a big hit with most dogs. Free food! *The rules for clicker conditioning are relatively simple: click first, then treat immediately after.* It's best to keep quiet during this process. You simply distract the dog from learning the click-signals-treat association by talking. Do the conditioning in a number of short sessions throughout the day. In this stage, don't ask for any specific behavior before the click. You can test your dog's understanding of the association by clicking at a time when your dog isn't expecting it and watching her reaction. You should see her become alert and come to you for her treat.

A small number of dogs, often herding breeds or dogs with flight-driven behavioral tendencies, display an initial fear reaction to the sound of the clicker. If a fear reaction occurs, don't give up hope. Many dogs can be successfully clicker trained given just a bit of extra effort. Try clicking from another room while your dog is eating. You might muffle the sound of the click by using the clicker from a pocket. Some people have had luck using the lid from a glass soft drink container (the sound is much softer). You could substitute another sound, like a soft whistle, if necessary. If your dog has an unpleasant initial reaction, you should still persist in finding a useful CR as it is the key to training using operant conditioning techniques.

One problem that may occur is a dog who is not food motivated. Food is by far the most convenient PR to use, but definitely not the only one. Before making the determination that food is not useful, I would make an effort to find some type of food that might be desirable to the dog. Be creative and try anything you can imagine. Cooked liver with garlic is almost always a hit. Also, be sure the dog is somewhat hungry. A free fed dog should have his access to food restricted prior to training. Dogs fed on a schedule might be given just a portion, rather than the entire meal, prior to training.

If you discover that your dog will absolutely not work for food, then you need to work hard to discover other PRs that you can use. Training toys, especially furry squeaky ones, can work well. The only time the dog has access to the toy should be during training. You can usually build desire for the toy by keeping it out of the dog's reach (possibly on top of the refrigerator). Several times during the day your should take the toy out and play with it yourself. Be loud and have fun! Many dogs, especially terriers, find this irresistible. If your dog expresses interest, great. However, don't let her play with the toy. Keep building the desire until your conditioning sessions. A reinforcement in this case might be to click and let the dog sniff the toy briefly before putting it in your pocket or hiding it behind your back.

Once the conditioning process is complete you have a wonderful tool to use in communicating with your dog. You can use your clicker to let your dog know that she is doing what you want. Dogs learn to try new behaviors or variations of behaviors in order to earn clicks and treats.

FREE SHAPING

I mentioned the concept of shaping earlier in describing how behaviors are trained and refined. Free shaping means that the dog is free to behave in any manner he chooses. From those behaviors offered, the trainer 'catches' and selectively reinforces the ones he or she would like to see repeated. In order to successfully free shape behavior the trainer needs to be prepared. During free shaping you will need the following: a dog, a quantity of irresistible primary reinforcers, a clicker, privacy, and patience. It's wise to put other dogs in a different place to avoid distractions. The main problem I have is that all the dogs want to be the one being trained and all start vying for my attention. Resolve to keep the environment stress-free and quiet during free shaping. Of all the necessary components, patience is absolutely the most important. Free shaping is about the dog trying out new behaviors. If you feel the need to give signals, prompts, commands, lures, etc., then free shaping will not happen. Resolve to steel yourself against offering any 'help' to the dog. Allow the dog the time and space to figure out for himself what leads to reinforcement and what doesn't.

Begin free shaping by having the clicker in your hand and the treats in an easily accessible place right next to you. It may help to give the dog some cue that a session is beginning. You could ask in a bright happy voice "ready for training?" Since your dog has already been conditioned to the clicker, usually just the sight of it is enough to signal that it's time for something good to happen. Your job is to closely observe your dog's behavior. However, don't scowl or project a 'serious' facial expression. Soften your features and maintain a pleasant expression.

You might have some idea of the target or goal behavior you want to work on, or you might simply observe the dog and pick a behavior at random to start reinforcing. The easiest behaviors to free shape are those which your dog has a natural desire and tendency to perform. Some dogs spin or jump easily and often, others use their paws quite frequently, others might vocalize quite a bit. *Pick a behavior for which the dog already has a preexisting tendency and you've just made your job much easier.* Shaping is about building behaviors by reinforcing the smallest of approximations or attempts that will lead to the ultimate goal behavior. If your goal or target behavior is 'speak' you would reinforce any sound at all, not wait for a full-blown bark. If you were thinking of training a 'high five', you would reinforce any foot movement, even slight shifting.

For my Golden Retriever, Sully, I free shaped the behavior of him putting his head on my knee and holding it there. I started by CTing him any time his head was close to my leg. Pretty quickly, he got the idea. I could tell he understood when he would repeat the reinforced behavior over and over. Then I 'upped the criteria' by making CT dependent on his actually touching my leg with his head. I didn't expect anything other than a quick bump at this point. Again, I could tell when he understood because he kept repeating the behavior. The next step was to only CT when he touched the top of my leg with his head. Then I 'upped the criteria' again by only CTing those responses where he kept his head on my leg at least 2 seconds. From there I could increase the duration required for CT. Shaping is always a matter of this shifting of criteria depending on the dog's behavior. Once the dog demonstrates an understanding of a gross approximation of the behavior, we redefine the requirements for reinforcement. It's very important to do this slowly and methodically. If I had jumped from step one (put your head near my leg) to step four (hold your head on my leg for 2 seconds) I would have been making the process unnecessarily difficult for my dog. Shaping should occur in small, easy steps so that the dog can be successful.

A small number of dogs are initially unwilling to freely offer behaviors. They may simply sit and stare at the trainer, waiting for a sign or signal. Often these dogs have been well-trained using traditional methods. Sometimes it is possible to outwait these rock-like creatures and reinforce any movement at all. If you are very observant you may be able to pick up on very small behaviors that can be reinforced. In one class we had a Sheltie who simply sat and stared at his trainer. We started reinforcing any slight ear twitch or movement. After a couple of sessions, he was doing a nice 'ears forward' show pose. For those dogs determined to wait until the next century for a cue, you may have to move around a bit to get them moving, then CT their movement. However, it's important to fade out your movement as quickly as possible so that the dog doesn't simply depend on it as a cue. There will be more suggestions on dealing with 'freezing' problems in the section on creativity.

Dogs 'throw' behaviors when they offer a string of actions very quickly. Some dogs offer so many behaviors in such a short time that it's nearly impossible to isolate a single one to reinforce. You might get a string that goes like this: sit, bark, sit up, lay down, jump, play bow, spin. The trainer with this type of dog needs to develop good timing and observational skills very quickly. Often you are reinforcing 3 or 4 behaviors after the one you intended. For this dog you need to choose large, easily observable behaviors to reinforce. You'll need to work on making your timing as fast and accurate as possible. The good news is that these dogs are usually very well-suited for clicker training. The ability and willingness to try and discard many behaviors very quickly is a good sign. These dogs are naturally creative and seem to enjoy the challenge of finding the reinforceable behavior.

Free shaping is an important exercise for both the dog and the trainer. It teaches the trainer a number of important skills. The trainer learns how to devise a plan to move from a gross initial approximation to a refined target behavior. Timing is learned through practice. Observational skills are sharpened. Most importantly, having patience and allowing the dog to work through the process are required. The dog learns that offering behaviors is a good thing that can lead to reinforcement. This is an important and powerful lesson for many dogs. They can learn to loosen up and be creative.

TRAINING GAME

An activity called the 'training game' is a common exercise for clicker trainers and in clicker classes. First described in Karen Pryor's *"Don't Shoot the Dog"* (a definite must read), the game is a fun and interesting way to introduce clicker training to novices. The game is basically free shaping using human subjects. Playing the game demonstrates the importance of proper timing. It also gives people an idea of how the animal feels during the training process.

To play the training game you need a clicker, some primary reinforcers, a trainer, and a subject. In my General Psychology classes I would often first demonstrate the game by being the trainer and asking for a volunteer subject. After that, I would get pairs of volunteers to play both roles. Start out by clicker conditioning, just as you would with a dog. For these games I usually use small, wrapped candies. However, any small desirable PR could be used. Condition the clicker by pairing the click with the treat. For humans you only need to do this a few times. We have the subject leave the room and the class decides on the behavior to be shaped. It's best to stick with large, obvious behaviors. The most common ones are: turning in a circle, sitting in a specific chair, doing jumping jacks, turning off the lights, writing your name on the chalkboard.

Before the game begins I explain the importance of reinforcing the smallest approximations of the target behavior. New trainers often want to wait until the full-blown behavior occurs before reinforcing. By explaining that click = information it is possible to get trainers to understand that they should be very generous with their clicks and treats. For example, if the target behavior is turning off the lights, the first clicks should be for being on the side of the room with the light switch or glancing in the direction of the switch. Once the subject is focused on the correct area they only get clicked for moving closer to the switch.

The subject is brought into the room and instructed to begin moving randomly around the room and listen for clicks. A click means that the subject is moving in the desired direction. The subject can come back after the click to collect each treat, or, to save time, the treats can be put into a pile to be collected at the end. (Don't try this with animals, only with humans. Animals must receive the treat after each click.) In the hundreds of times I've played the game, I've seen some of the same responses from subjects over and over. First of all, they become fixated on the trainer. They watch very closely for any sign or signal. This happens with dogs as well as with people. Also, especially at first, human subjects tend to get stuck. They get clicked, then they stop and start trying to reason out why they got clicked. I always tell people at this stage "stop thinking, start moving". Higher mental functions are not an advantage in this game, in fact, they tend to interfere.

In general, subjects figure out their target behavior within a few minutes. The ease with which this occurs depends on the skill and timing of the trainer. If this is done in front of a class, the class will often be able to pinpoint a click that was too slow, a missed opportunity, or an unintentional reinforcement of the wrong behavior. These are very instructive experiences. The class is also very tense and definitely pulling for the subject to get the reinforceable behavior. I always ask subjects to describe their feelings during the game. Often they report confusion, especially with a novice trainer. This is a very useful exercise for putting the subject "in their dog's paws" and helping them to understand training from the dog's perspective. All dog trainers should have the experience of being both the trainer and the subject in this game.

An interesting variation of the training game is to add a non-reinforcement marker (NRM). The purpose of the NRM is to tell the subject that she is performing a behavior that will never be reinforced. This added information can be very useful. Think of the 'hot/cold' game that kids play. The click is 'hot', it means you're doing the right thing. Adding a 'cold' signal makes it faster and

easier for the subject to narrow down possible behaviors. You can choose
any signal for a NRM. I tend to use 'wrong' said in a neutral voice. For
humans, you can simply explain the meaning of the signal. Dogs
need to be conditioned to understand it. I'll explain how to do
that in the section on adding cues and signals.

CREATIVITY SESSIONS

For dogs and handlers who are having trouble
with free shaping, there are several creativity exercises
that can be helpful. These exercises are very useful for
dogs who freeze and simply don't offer any behaviors.

1. 101 things to do with a box.

Actually, it doesn't have to be a box, it can be
any object that is not dangerous to your dog. The more
intriguing or unusual the object the better. For this exercise
you're trying to get your dog to offer any behaviors at all.
Be prepared with your clicker and treats handy. Put out the
object you'd like your dog to explore. Now CT ANY interaction
your dog has with the object. CT a glance, CT a sniff, CT a touch,
CT a bump, CT a circle.... The purpose of this exercise is to get the
dog to loosen up and start offering behaviors. It also gives the trainer an
opportunity to practice observation and timing. What should you do if your dog keeps
repeating a specific behavior? Let's say you CTd your dog for bumping the box with his
nose. Now he's pushing the box around the room by his nose. Keep CTing as long as the
dog is engaged and you're both enjoying it. Once you're tired of that behavior, you can quit
reinforcing it and move on to something else. When you do this you'll probably see an
extinction burst, but it passes if it isn't reinforced.

2. Try something else.

Once dogs start to understand shaping, you can make the game a bit more difficult
in order to challenge them and keep their attention. In the 'try something else' game, the
dog is given CT for any behavior that's different from the last one. In this version of shaping,
repetition is not reinforced, trying out new behaviors is. If your dog offers a sit you would
CT that the first time, then wait for anything else. She might lay down next, CT that. Then

wait again. She might scratch an ear and you could CT that. The idea here is that the dog cannot rely on one or two behaviors to earn CT, she must keep trying something else.

3. Give me something new.

This is probably the most challenging of the creativity games. Don't try this until your dog understands free shaping very well. It's a great game for dogs who get bored easily. Many dogs learn a few behaviors very quickly and tend to repeat those over and over. Some dogs put together their own repertoire of favorites. You get out the clicker and treats and your dog goes into the act. One of my dogs will do the following if I just stand there watching her: sit, speak, down, head down, jump up, front, bump me. In 'give me something new' none of those old behaviors are reinforced. Let your dog run through the act and wait patiently. Your dog might start to get frustrated because nothing is working.

Remain calm and smile at your dog. You might want to offer a bit of quiet encouragement to keep trying, but keep it to a minimum. The first time I did this with my Lab, Katie, she became quite frustrated. Katie's not incredibly creative (except in the obedience ring!) Finally, in what seemed like desperation, she jumped up and bumped my mouth with her muzzle. She had just invented 'kiss' and got CTd.

TARGETING

Targeting is one of the most useful behaviors your dog can learn. Targeting is a basic foundation skill. The ability to target makes teaching many complex behaviors much easier (more on this in the target tricks section). A target can be any object that you teach your dog to move towards. The most commonly used targets are a touch stick and your hand. To begin teaching targeting you will need a target, clicker, and treats.

Touch stick. A touch stick can be any of a variety of objects. A dowel rod, wooden spoon, or venetian blind rod can be used. It's important that one end of the stick be a contrasting color. This is the part the dog will touch. An easy way to accomplish this is to wrap some colored tape around the end of the stick. The length of the stick depends on the size of your dog and the types of tricks you would like to teach. I use a 2-foot stick for my retrievers. To start, you need to practice holding the touch stick and clicker while giving treats. It feels somewhat awkward at first, but is not impossible. It just takes a bit of practice and coordination. I'm right-handed and I hold the stick in my right palm and the clicker in the same hand between my thumb and forefinger. That leaves my left hand free to give treats.

Our goal is to teach the dog to touch the end of the touch stick with her nose. This is a shaping exercise. Hold the stick somewhere in front of your dog's face at nose level. If she even glances at it, CT. Many dogs will sniff the stick. Make sure you catch this and CT it. If your dog ignores the stick, wave it around a bit to try and get her attention. Resist the urge to touch your dog with the stick. All this does is teach the dog to hold still while you wave the stick around. If your dog is still showing no interest in the stick you can 'cheat' a bit to get her started. Put a dab of peanut butter on the end of the stick. When your dog approaches to lick/sniff, you can click. The peanut butter serves as the treat. Continue this training by raising your requirements for CT as the dog begins looking at, sniffing, or moving towards the stick. Move slowly. Make sure your dog understands each step before you move on. Here's a typical example of how you might shape the touch stick. Be aware that your dog will not follow this pattern exactly. Some dogs may act as though the stick is invisible while others may run to it and start touching it immediately. This is just an example to give you an idea of how and when to raise criteria for reinforcement.

1. Dog glances at stick. You CT (Click & Treat).
2. Same.
3. Same.
4. Same.
5. Same. After about 5 repetitions, you can move on to the next step.
6. Dog glances at stick. You smile and wait. Dog may be surprised that a previously reinforced behavior did not work. At this point the dog may repeat the behavior or try something else.

7. Dog turns entire head towards stick. You CT.

8. Same.

9. Same.

10. Same.

11. Same.

12. Dog turns entire head towards stick. You smile and wait.

13. Dog moves head forwards towards stick. You CT.

14. Same.

15. Same.

16. Same.

17. Same.

18. Raise requirements here. Wait for something more, such as dog actually getting up and moving towards the stick.

Every shaping session is a unique experience. What you do depends on what the dog does. The only way to get a good feel for shaping is through practice and experience.

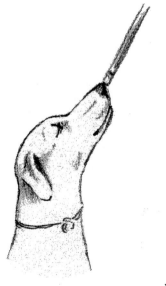

Work on shaping the touch stick in short sessions several times a day. Most dogs will have the concept within a week. Make sure that you hold the stick in different places around the dog during the shaping process. Otherwise, you might end up training your dog to only touch when the stick is 2 inches to her right. Once your dog will reliably touch the stick whenever she sees it, you can add the cue word 'touch' right before she touches. There will be more specifics on adding cues and signals in the next section.

Hand target. You can teach your dog to touch the palm of your hand or your fist in the same way you shaped the touch stick. When shaping a hand target be careful how you hold your hand. If you hold it in a manner similar to a hand signal that the dog already knows, you may be confusing your dog.

Other targets. You can teach your dog to touch any target. Using a clear margarine lid or film canister as a target can be very useful for both obedience and agility exercises. Start by holding the target, just as you did with the touch stick. Then put the target on the ground in front of you. Then you can move the target further away and send the dog towards it. Each time you move the location of the target you will need to lower your requirements for reinforcement, then slowly raise them again. The subject of target tricks will be discussed further in its own section.

ADDING CUES AND SIGNALS

Initial cues. Contrary to more traditional methods of dog training, commands or cues are not introduced at the beginning of training. You won't begin using cues until the behavior is being performed consistently and reliably. This avoids the 'sit, sit, sit, sit, SIT!' syndrome that so many people display. Adding the cue too early can confuse the dog. Strangely, it also convinces the trainer that the dog knows the exercise and is simply choosing not to respond. It's much better to be quiet and let the dog learn the behavior thoroughly, then add the cue. Gary Wilkes says that you shouldn't add the cue until you would bet $20 that the dog will perform the behavior. This is an excellent guideline to follow.

Let's use the target stick as an example. After several weeks of practice you are fairly confident that when you hold out the stick your dog will touch it. At this point you can add the cue 'touch' just as your dog begins the behavior. Then CT as usual. By constantly pairing the cue word with the presentation of the stick, your dog will learn that the term 'touch' signals the opportunity to touch the stick.

Changing cues. Trainers often want to change cues, or add another cue for the same behavior. You may want to add a hand signal to an already existing verbal cue. Changing or adding cues is a fairly simple process. Just remember that you need to use the new cue first, then the old cue. Over time, your dog will come to perform the behavior on the new cue alone. Let's say you decide to change your cue for the touch stick from 'touch' to 'stick'. The pattern would be: 'Stick'...'Touch' CT. Over time you can fade out the 'touch' cue as the dog performs on the 'stick' cue alone.

Non-reinforcement marker. A NRM is a signal to your dog that reinforcement is not forthcoming for the behavior he is performing. This signal has to be conditioned, just like any other cue. John Fisher (a noted British behaviorist) talked and wrote at great length about the use of NRMs. He said that the opposite of reinforcement is not punishment, but non-reinforcement. Think about a time when you expected something reinforcing but didn't receive it. You probably didn't enjoy the experience. If you've ever been expecting a paycheck and didn't receive it, you know the feeling I'm talking about.

A dog needs to understand the click-treat connection and the shaping process before he can understand the concept of non-reinforcement. You can choose any signal for a NRM, but several are very common. These include the word 'wrong' and the universal 'uhn, uhn' sound. It's important that the signal be given in a neutral tone. This is not meant to be punishing for the dog, simply a way to convey information. At first, you need to make it clear to your dog in a fairly dramatic fashion that he has just lost his opportunity for reinforcement. Let's say that during a shaping session he starts sniffing a particularly fragrant corner, and that this is nowhere close to the target behavior. Give the NRM, take your clicker and your treats, and dramatically walk out of the room. Once your dog becomes aware that the 'human hot dog machine' is no longer operating and comes looking for you, go back and start again. Remember to always clearly give the NRM before you remove the possibility of reinforcement. After repeated pairings, the signal alone should be enough to reorient the dog to the task at hand. So what if you make your dramatic exit and your dog continues sniffing in the corner? Next time you train, set up the situation so that the unwanted behavior is less likely to occur.

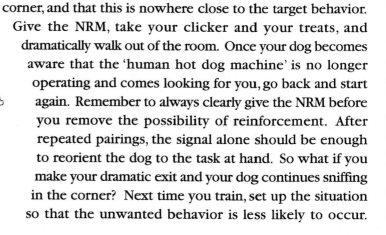

Think of the NRM as a way of saying "wrong, try something else". You'd like for the dog to do something other than the activity that he's engaged in.

You don't want the dog to stop trying to earn +R (Positive Reinforcement), simply to stop going down a dead-end behavioral path.

The NRM can save you lots of time during shaping by narrowing down the realm of reinforceable behaviors. The NRM should come to mean "not that, try again".

REINFORCEMENT SCHEDULES

Continuous reinforcement. As I stated earlier, you should use continuous reinforcement throughout the learning stage of any particular behavior. Every time the behavior is performed, it should be reinforced. Until a behavior is solid and reliable, the dog needs the information that reinforcement provides.

Variable reinforcement. Once a behavior is well-learned, variable reinforcement (in particular, variable ratio reinforcement) is a good way to maintain the behavior. An easy way to start VR is with 2fers and 3fers. Rather than reinforcing each behavior, you now reinforce every two or three behaviors. VR keeps a behavior occurring at a high, consistent level. In continuous reinforcement, subjects can sometimes get lazy. They might not perform well on each behavior because they expect that reinforcement will always be available. With VR, however, there's an element of surprise involved. The behavior may or may not be reinforced on any particular try.

The classic example of continuous vs. variable reinforcement can be illustrated by comparing a soda machine to a slot machine. A soda machine operates on a continuous reinforcement schedule (barring any unfortunate glitches). You put in your money and you get your soda. A slot machine operates on a variable ratio reinforcement schedule. You can never predict when the payoff will occur. It could be after one pull or after one hundred. Yet people persist in feeding money into a slot machine. If the soda machine doesn't give you a payoff fairly quickly, you tend to give up. Once a behavior is well-learned, trainers should strive to be more like slot machines than like soda machines. We typically want our dogs to perform behaviors even when they will not always be reinforced. It's possible to move to a very thin reinforcement schedule, but it must be done slowly and carefully. If being maintained on 2fers and 3fers you can try for a higher number of unreinforced repetitions. Keep in mind that the dog should always be guessing. Sometimes give two reinforcements in a row. Don't fall into a predictable pattern. Also, don't always make it harder to gain reinforcement. This can be discouraging. Strive to be surprising and variable. This will keep your dog's attention and interest.

CHAINING BEHAVIORS

A number of tricks described in this book require the construction of behavior chains. A chain consists of two or more behaviors that make up a desired sequence. For example, teaching your dog to get you a soda from the refrigerator is a behavior chain. You put together a number of specific behaviors (go to the fridge, open the door, pick up a soda, etc.) into one sequence performed on cue.

Chains are taught by breaking them down into their smallest components and training each of those separately. Once each part of the chain has been learned, the behaviors can be put together. At first you put two of the chained behaviors together, then add more as your dog learns to perform the sequence correctly.

Many behaviors are best trained by backchaining. In backchaining you ask for the very last behavior in the chain, then reinforce that. Then you ask for the last two behaviors in the chain, and reinforce after the last one. The dog is always working towards the reinforcer. More and more behaviors are added—one at a time—to the front of the chain. For the soda trick you would start with the very last behavior, having the dog give you the soda. Reinforce that behavior. Then add the next to the last behavior, bringing your soda from the kitchen and handing it to you. Once the dog is performing these two behaviors, you can add a third, getting the soda out of the fridge. Continue building the backchain until you have incorporated all of the component behaviors.

3 *Tricks*

a. Target Tricks

b. Paw Tricks

c. Retrieve Tricks

d. Miscellaneous Tricks

e. Presentation & Costumes

CHAPTER 3: TRICKS

Remember, tricks are meant to be fun for both you and your dog. Please be aware of your dog's safety and physical limitations at all times. It's your responsibility to look out for your friend's well-being. If you have any doubts about your dog's ability to perform a trick, check with your veterinarian before continuing. For the more active tricks always be aware of your dog's footing and the nature of the ground/floor on which your dog must land. Repeated jumping on concrete can be very damaging to your dog's bones and joints. Wet or slick floors can lead to falls and injuries. Always be cautious with your dog's health and safety.

TARGET TRICKS

As I've said before, targeting is an absolutely essential fundamental skill. A number of tricks are simply variations on targeting. Once the dog performs 'touch' reliably on cue, you can try any of the following target tricks.

Bow. Always cute. Begin with your dog standing. Take your target stick and place it on the floor between your dog's front feet, moving it back just slightly under the chest. The dog's nose should follow the stick and her front legs will bend back. CT as soon as the bending motion starts. Work towards a more pronounced bow. Remember, be generous with CT at first. Your target behavior here is to have the dog's elbows on the ground and rump in the air. Once you get the position you can extend the time the dog holds it by withholding the click for a bit longer. If the dog moves out of position before you click, simply start again. Increase duration very slowly.

You may need to be very quick to catch your dog before his rump hits the ground as well as his elbows. Dogs who understand 'down' may have trouble with bow. If your dog insists on laying down completely try putting a rolled-up towel in front of his back feet. When he hits this he might raise his rear-end. You might also use a hand to steady your dog's tuck-up area (don't apply pressure, just hold your hand still) the first few times you try this.

Also, be careful with your cue word here. 'Down' and 'bow' sound very similar. You might use a different cue such as 'stretch'.

Crawl. Begin with your dog in a sphinx down (not on either hip, rear end centered over back legs). Place target stick directly under dog's nose and move it forward just a few inches. You want the stick forward just enough so that your dog has to move her head to touch it. CT any forward movement towards the stick. If your dog stands up it's because the stick is too far away. Keep it close to your dog's head and move it forward very, very slowly as you encourage your dog to touch. Don't try to add distance too quickly as this encourages your dog to get up. You can make progress in inches, not in feet.

Show me your belly. This can be a useful behavior for grooming and vet exams. You want your dog to roll over on his back with his belly exposed. With this trick and with 'roll over' never force your dog. Dogs with hip or back problems may be unable to perform this behavior.

The quickest and easiest way to elicit this behavior is by using a food lure. Have your dog in a down. Encourage him to lean to one side by moving the lure beside your dog's head, then CT. When your dog will do this comfortably, encourage him to lean a bit further each time. You can do this by moving the lure slowly up and around your dog's shoulder. His nose will turn to follow the lure, and his body will turn to the side. Keep doing this until he is flat on his back. A belly rub while in this position is a good reinforcer.

Roll over. Teach this in the same was as described above for 'show me your belly'. However, instead of stopping while your dog is flat on his back, continue the circle with the food lure. Some dogs resist this behavior at first, but get better at it once they understand what you want. Go slowly and never force your dog over.

Spin. Start with your dog standing in front of you. Hold the stick at nose height. You don't want your dog to hold her head up. Move it very slowly to one side and tell your dog to touch. CT any head turn in the direction of the stick. Over time raise your requirements for more and more movement to one side. First CT for 1/8 of the circle, then for 1/4, etc. etc. Use the stick to lead your dog in a tight circle. A cute cue for this trick is "chase your tail". This is a very enjoyable behavior for some dogs. In fact, the trick may be to get obsessive tail-chasers to stop spinning!

Reverse. Just what it sounds like. You'll ask your dog to spin in the opposite direction. Most dogs have a preferred direction to spin. This may be a bit harder for your dog if this is her non-preferred side.

Head down. This trick is preferred by the more laid-back canines. Start with the dog in a down. Put your target stick on the floor directly under the dog's chin and ask for a 'touch'. From there you simply build up duration slowly over time. Once your dog is reliably touching the stick simply hold it still and delay the CT for a second or so. Then move up to two or three seconds, etc. If your dog raises his head before the click, just start over, no CT for that trial. My cue phrase for this behavior is "take a nap".

Sit up. Dogs with back or hip problems may have trouble with this one. Sit up can be especially difficult for dogs with long backs such as Dachshunds and Corgis. Start with the dog in a sit. For dogs with balance problems, you can have them sit with their backs against a wall or in a corner for support. Hold the target stick up just enough above the dog's head so the dog must lift her front feet slightly off the ground, then CT. As your dog becomes steady raise the target stick higher. Keep the stick centered over your dog's head so she doesn't move forward in an attempt to touch it. You want your dog lifting straight up from the sit and staying balanced on her haunches.

Stand up. Instead of balancing on his haunches, your dog will balance on his hind legs in this stand. You can start with your dog in a sit or a four-legged stand. Hold up the target stick over her head and encourage her to raise up and touch it. Keep the stick still as your dog reaches for it to discourage jumping and to encourage steadiness. Keep moving the stick the higher and higher as your trials continue, until she must stand on her two back feet to reach it. Over time, CT for longer and steadier stands.

Walk backwards/dance. Once your dog can 'stand up' you can move on to more complex behaviors. Your dog needs to be very steady on her two back feet before she can attempt to either 'walk backwards' or to 'dance'. Use the target stick to train these behaviors. With your dog in a steady stand on her back feet, move the target stick very slowly backwards, over her head. CT any slight movement your dog makes backwards. Most dogs find it easiest to hop back. Gradually increase your criteria for CT. Be sure to keep the target stick low, so your dog doesn't try to jump to touch it.

For 'dance' you will want to move your dog into a 'spin' while she's standing on her back feet. Follow the previous instructions for 'spin'. For both 'walk backwards' and 'dance' give your dog plenty of time. Also, allow her to drop back down on all four legs when she feels the need to. You don't want her to lose her balance and fall or strain a muscle.

Jump. Hold the target stick just high enough so your dog must do a little hop in order to touch it. Over time you can move the stick higher and higher. Be sure that your dog is athletic enough for the height you require and also that he's on solid footing.

Bounce. This is a favorite of poodles and Jack Russell Terriers! Bouncing is simply repeating jump over and over. This can be very impressive in smaller, athletic dogs. Again, be careful of height and footing. A slip on landing could cause an injury.

Lights on & off. Service dogs are often trained to turn room lights on and off for their owners. Your dog can learn to perform this same service. However, you may have to put up with claw marks and/or drool (depending on whether your dog uses her paws or mouth) around your light switches. You might want to put plastic protectors on the wall around your switches for this trick. Or you might do what service dog trainers do: construct a practice switchplate for training purposes.

To train this behavior you can use a touch stick to direct your dog to the light switch. Once your dog is reliably touching the switch you can encourage pawing or nosing to move the switch up or down. Typically, dogs find it easier to nose up and paw down. With practice your dog will get good at manipulating the switch.

Flashlight/laser. With both of these beams, be careful of your dog's eyes. Never shine a light, especially a laser, directly into the dog's face. Some dogs naturally follow light beams; others seem to not even see them. When training a flashlight target it's best to use a small light with a concentrated beam. You'll need to work in a darkened room. Turn on the flashlight and move the beam around on the floor in front of your dog. To get started you might drop treats into the light beam and then click as the dog picks up the treats. Make sure to move the beam around from trial to trial. You don't want your dog only moving towards the beam when it's in one particular spot, say, six inches to her left. Small laser pointers are also fun targets. Instead of the usual light, they emit a red dot. You can teach your dog to go to this dot in the same way you train the flashlight. Once your dog seems to understand the concept of touching the light, you can use the beam to direct her to toys or other objects you'd like her to touch.

Touch this. 'Touch this' is simply applying the concept of touch to any number of possible objects. My favorites are children's toys. I've used a toy piano and a toy that makes animal sounds when certain buttons are pushed.

I trained each of my dogs to touch a different button on the animal sounds toy. I did this by holding the toy in front of me, facing the dog, and only reinforcing touches to a specific button. Touching other buttons was ignored, and those behaviors quickly extinguished. Katie only got reinforced for hitting the button on the bottom–the pig, in honor of her appetite. Sully only got reinforced for hitting the button on the top–the chicken, which is somewhat descriptive of his personality. I tell people that these are their impersonations of barnyard animals.

You could also use a target stick initially to direct the dog to the toy or object. Then fade out the stick and simply point.

Move here/move there. You can use targeting to get your dog to move to different locations. The target stick, small plastic target, or light beam are good tools for this behavior. They allow you to send the dog some distance away.

In the Utility class in competitive obedience there is an exercise called Directed Jumping. In the first part of the exercise the dog must perform a go-out: run across the ring directly away from the handler until told to turn and sit. Many trainers use a food target to train their dogs for this exercise. They put food on the wall/ring gate/floor where they want the dog to go. One problem with this method is that the dog gets to the other side of the ring and starts sniffing around for the food, even when it is not present. Instead of actually putting the PR out, you can put out a target instead. Once the dog gets to the target, CT. The target can be faded over time by hiding part of it under a mat if using a stick, or by cutting it into smaller and smaller pieces if using a plastic lid or paper plate.

When training for agility you may also find targeting very useful. Targets can be used to teach the dog to go away from you and perform behaviors. Often in agility you would like the dog to move ahead and take a series of jumps or obstacles. Our dogs can move much faster than we can and it's important to save time on an agility course. You can encourage the dog to move ahead of you by putting the target beyond a jump or obstacle and sending your dog to the target, then CT. You can add jumps or obstacles to the series as your dog demonstrates an understanding of the exercise.

Targets can also be used in agility to teach your dog to slow down and touch contact zones (areas at the base of certain obstacles that your dog must touch). You can use a target stick to show the dog where she needs to touch. Or, you might use a clear plastic margarine lid or clear small film canister placed on the spot you want your dog to stop and touch. It might help to use a bit of double-sided tape to hold the target in place. When starting this type of target training make sure your dog is moving very slowly. A dog running full speed won't even notice the target. Be clear in pointing out the target and giving the 'touch' cue. CT immediately. Stay close at first and as your dog gains confidence you can give the cue from further and further away.

Look here/look there. Rather than having the dog actually move his body in a specific direction, you might just want to get your dog to move his head and look. You can use a target or target stick to get the dog to look up, down, left, and right. You can then add cues for each of these directions. A cute cue for looking down is something like "Have you been a bad dog?" Then the dog hangs his head and looks at the floor. You could also teach a complete motion up & down for 'yes' and side to side for 'no'. Then ask your dog questions. For example, all 'yes' questions could begin with the cue words "Are you". "Are you a good dog?" "Are you ready to go home?" "Are you having fun?" All 'no' questions could begin with the cue words "Do you". "Do you like broccoli?" "Do you need a bath?" "Do you want to go to the vet?"

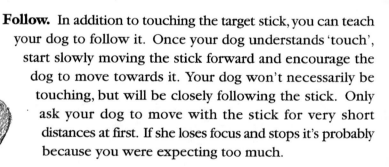

Follow. In addition to touching the target stick, you can teach your dog to follow it. Once your dog understands 'touch', start slowly moving the stick forward and encourage the dog to move towards it. Your dog won't necessarily be touching, but will be closely following the stick. Only ask your dog to move with the stick for very short distances at first. If she loses focus and stops it's probably because you were expecting too much.

Some trainers have used the target stick to teach heeling. Hold the stick where you want your dog's nose to be and move forward a step or two, then CT. You can increase the number of steps and complexity of your movements (turns, changes of pace) over time.

Follow me. This is an application of following. Hold the target stick behind your back with the end at your dog's nose height. Encourage your dog to move behind you to touch, CT. Once your dog will do this confidently take a step forward encouraging your dog to follow. Over time increase the number of steps you take while asking your dog to follow directly behind you. This behavior would be a nice addition to a freestyle (dog/handler dance) routine. I've also used it when in very close quarters at dog shows, street fairs, etc.

Circle me. This is simply applying 'follow' so that the dog makes a circle around you. You could use it in a dance routine, especially square dancing. Start with the target stick directly in front of you with the end at your dog's nose height. The dog should be standing in front of you facing towards the side. Start moving the stick and encourage the dog to follow. CT your dog's efforts. When the stick is behind your back you'll need to switch hands (this can be difficult for those of us lacking in coordination!) You may want to teach this in both directions and use different cue words for each.

Figure 8. For this trick you will be using the target stick to lead your dog into two intersecting circles. This behavior uses the same motions that your dog performs in 'spin' and 'reverse'. You are just slowing them down and putting them together. Always start your dog circling in the same direction on the figure 8. Use the target stick to lead your dog into one circle, then into the other.

Twist. In this behavior the dog weaves between and around the handler's legs in a figure 8 pattern. This trick can be difficult for short people with large dogs or for tall people with small dogs. Start with your dog on your left side. Encourage the dog to move forward then between your legs to the back. It's easiest to use a food lure, possibly cheese, hot dog, or peanut butter on the end of your target stick for this trick (it saves your back some wear and tear). Click and let your dog have the treat after this initial step. Once your dog performs this behavior willingly the next step is to get the dog to move around the outside of your right leg to back in front of you. Practice this portion until your dog performs it confidently. Now you're going to repeat the exercise with the dog going between your legs and circling the left leg, ending up back at your left side. If this all sounds quite complicated, simply think of it as a figure 8 for your dog with your legs as posts. Breaking the behavior down into a number of small sections and CTing after each will help your dog learn.

Ring a bell. I've taught several dogs to indicate when they need to go outside by ringing a bell. This is a fairly easy procedure. Attach a small bell (I use the kind they sell for bird cages) to a length of rope/string. Loop the rope over the doorknob on the door the dog uses to go outside. Every time you let the dog out encourage her to touch the bell (either with her nose or her paw, most prefer the nose), then CT before opening the door. Most dogs start to touch the bell on their own very quickly. Whenever this happens, no matter what you're doing, immediately CT and let the dog outside. Usually, the problem is that the dog enjoys this trick so much that she rings the bell all the time, whether she really needs to go outside or not. Smart dog! If this occurs simply put the bell away except for those times when you're willing to CT and let her out.

PAW TRICKS

Some dogs have a natural affinity for using their paws. If they had thumbs we'd be in great trouble! Many dogs use their paws in ways we wish they wouldn't—like scratching and digging. One of my favorite canines is Java, a Bernese Mountain dog. Java loves to give you 'death claw' whenever he can, grabbing at an arm or leg and raking his nails across your body. (He's not trying to hurt anyone, he just has big, strong paws that he likes to use). Paw tricks can take advantage of these tendencies and put them to a more acceptable use. Even dogs who don't normally use their paws for anything other than walking can be taught some very cute paw tricks.

Most of the paw tricks are variations on the same targeting theme. Instead of touching a target with his nose, you're now asking the dog to touch the target with his paw. Dogs can get confused at first by this distinction. Use clearly different signals and cues for paw tricks than the ones you used for target tricks.

I suggest teaching the paw tricks in the order indicated, as they go from the simplest to the most complex. Each builds on the foundation of those previously taught.

Shake. A tried and true favorite. What you're asking your dog to do is simply put his paw in your hand when you present it palm up. Your upturned palm is the signal as well as the target for this behavior. Most people add a verbal cue "shake hands" or "give paw" as well. You can 'shake' either or both paws, but to start, choose one and stick with it until your dog understands the concept. Also, always offer the same target hand to avoid confusion.

There are a number of ways to elicit paw shaking behavior. Any of these may take a number of repetitions before your dog 'gets it'. You may have to try more than one method. You could start by reinforcing any movement of the paw off the ground, rather than going for the actual touching of the palm at first. This can be done purely with free shaping, but may take some time. Simply watch closely and CT whenever the paw moves, even if only a fraction of an inch. Over time, you can reinforce for more and more movement. Then you can add in the target of your upturned palm. Hold it out as your dog moves his paw, and reinforce for moving the paw closer and closer to your palm.

If your dog seems willing to sit like a statue rooted to the ground until the end of time you may need to try other options. You might hold out a treat to one side so that your dog moves slightly off balance to reach for it. When this occurs a paw will probably shift. You can click for that, then give the treat.

Another method would be to start with your upturned palm very low, practically on the ground. Then tickle the back of your dog's leg with your other hand (also holding the clicker) until he shifts it. At that point you can slide your palm under the foot, then CT. This tickle and slide method may take a number of trials before your dog starts to offer paw movement on his own.

You can manually place the dog's paw on your palm and shake, then CT. As with any method which involves manipulation or luring, a number of repetitions may be necessary before your dog offers the behavior on his own.

Almost all dogs learn some variation of shake given a bit of time and effort. Remember to have patience. This is the fun stuff!

High 5. Rather than putting a paw in your upturned palm, the high 5 involves reaching up to touch your hand with a paw. Imagine giving a 'stop' signal, arm extended, fingers pointing upwards, palm facing the dog. Be warned owners of very short-legged dogs like Corgis, Basset Hounds, and Dachshunds, this can be quite difficult, if not impossible, due to their structure. Go for the 'low 5' instead.

Once your dog has mastered 'shake', you can transfer that 'targeting with a paw' behavior. Start moving your hand into different positions so that your dog has to work a bit harder to touch it with his paw. Change the tilt and orientation of your hand. Try moving your hand to one side and at a slight angle. CT whenever your dog attempts to touch your hand with his paw. Over time, move your hand higher and higher, turning your palm to face the dog. The most comfortable height for 'high 5' is around your dog's shoulder height. You can do even higher 5s, but your dog must learn to first sit up, then give the 5 (another possibility for short-legged dogs). This is a behavior chain as previously described.

Other 5. Once you've mastered the 'high 5' with one paw, you can work on the 'other 5'. Use the opposite hand for a signal. You can expect a number of responses using the wrong paw at first, as this is what you've taught. Your dog will now need to distinguish between your hand signals (the same, only a different side) and offer the same response, but with the other paw. This can be a difficult switch for some animals. I imagine them thinking "just when I thought I understood..." You'll go through the same process in training 'other 5' as you did for 'high 5'. However, try to make it as distinctly different as possible for your dog. Train it in a new environment. Hold the target hand very far to the other side to discourage the dog from trying to reach it with the wrong paw. Don't punish responses with the wrong paw, use your NRM or ignore them, but encourage your dog to keep trying. This exercise is called a discrimination task by psychologists. Your dog has to learn the difference between two very similar cues and it can be quite difficult for some animals. As always, have patience and keep trying. This is not an impossible task, and most animals seem to enjoy showing off their discrimination skills once they've been learned.

High 10. Now you can get fancy with your paw tricks. In the 'high 10' your dog must place both front paws on both of your palms at the same time. In order to do this your dog must sit up on his hindquarters or stand up on his back legs first. Both of these were described in the 'target tricks' section earlier. Your first step in 'high 10' training is to teach your dog to move quickly into one of these positions.

Because you need both hands free to give the cue, you can't use the clicker as a marker for this behavior. This is one of the times when a verbal secondary reinforcer such as "Yes!", "Great!", or "Excellent!" is useful. The first few times you give the 'high 10' signal your dog will probably respond with only one paw. Verbally encourage your dog to move the other paw as well. At first, mark (with your verbal CR) and treat any trial in which both feet move. Over time, become more demanding in determining reinforceable behaviors (up your criteria).

I precede a signal for the 'high 10' with another signal to alert my dog. I clap my hands together once, then put both palms forward and ask for a '10'. This early signal (clap) allows my dog to move into the sit up or stand position and prepare for the behavior. This warning signal evolved fairly naturally over the course of training this behavior.

*Once you mastered the 'high 5', 'other 5', and 'high 10' you can put together a sequence demonstrating all three behaviors. This is an excellent demonstration of discrimination training. As time goes on, only reinforce quick and accurate responses to all three signals. Then you'll have a dog who can play 'patty-cake'.

47.

Wave. This is for those of you who fondly remember the original 'Lassie' television program. At the end of each show Lassie would sit and wave good-bye. To teach 'wave' you need to teach your dog to move his paw in the same way as for a 'high 5'. Once he performs this behavior reliably you'll begin to 'fade' the target (your hand). Start CTing responses in which the paw is held up, but doesn't touch your hand. Of course, this will be confusing to your dog at first (another discrimination task). You can give the same signal as for a 'high 5', but move your hand back slightly so your dog's paw doesn't touch. Over time give the signal from further and further away. I slowly change the signal to more of a 'wave' motion with my hand, bending my fingers up and down several times.

Tap. The idea for 'tap' came to me because of the story of Clever Hans. In psychology, the story of Clever Hans is widely reported and goes like this: There was a man who claimed that he had a very smart horse. In fact, this horse (Hans) was so smart that his owner claimed Hans could solve arithmetic problems. Indeed, it seemed from observation that Hans could solve math problems. When given a problem Hans would tap out the correct answer with his hoof. Of course, many people were skeptical of this ability. However, no one could find any explanation for the amazing mathematical abilities the horse had. He was always right! Asked to give answers to questions such as "what's 3 + 6?" or "4 x 2 equals what?" Hans would patiently tap out the correct responses. Those who observed Hans at work stated that the owner gave no cues or commands to the horse. A test was devised in which the owner would not be present when Hans was questioned. It was discovered that Hans could not answer questions when his owner was not there. Closer observation revealed that the owner was giving very subtle, unintentional cues. He held his breath while Hans was counting, and released it on the correct response. His brow was tense and furrowed during counting, and relaxed once the correct response was reached. Hans had picked up on these cues and was using them to tell him when to stop tapping. So, while Hans was not a math whiz, he was still a very observant animal.

After talking about Clever Hans in one of my psychology classes a student brought me a tape of a dog who supposedly could count. He would indicate his answers by barking. Like Hans, he was amazingly accurate. Also, like Hans, his owner was giving an unintentional, subtle cue. She would lightly tap her hand on her leg with each bark until the right answer was reached, then hold the hand still. Her dog was using this as a cue to stop barking.

These are examples of accidental learning. However, we can certainly train our animals to respond to very subtle cues. There are a number of ways in which a foot tap could be used in tricks. Show off your dog's mathematical abilities. You could have the next canine version of Clever Hans!

You can begin training this trick by using a target such as a margarine lid or paper plate. Decide which foot you will be concentrating on. Be consistent. Make it easy by choosing the one your dog seems to prefer. You can approach the problem from several ways, depending on your dog's level of training with paw tricks and targeting. You might use free shaping. CT any interaction the dog has with the target, and eventually narrow it down to touching the target with the foot. Then you can wait for multiple touches before you CT. A 'keep going' signal could be introduced at this point. Choose something that will look fairly natural for the finished trick, but exaggerate it during training to make sure your dog is aware of it. Head nodding, finger movement, or even tapping your own foot are examples. When you stop giving the signal, CT. Soon your dog will learn to stop when the signal ends.

You could approach this behavior from another angle and institute a 'stop' signal that you give immediately before CT. Something as simple as a loud exhale before each CT will become a signal for your dog to stop tapping. This removes the need for a 'keep going' signal.

If your dog has learned paw tricks and targeting fairly well, your job teaching 'tap' is much easier. Point out the target and give your dog her 'paw' signal. CT for any attempt to touch the target, and shape for quicker, more precise touches.

One variation on 'tap' is having your dog touch your foot with her paw. Your foot becomes the target. Just hold out your foot and give your 'tap' signal. CT when your dog attempts to touch your foot with her paw. This is fairly a simple variation to teach, but beware, it can be dangerous for bare legs. You might end up with scratches in the process of teaching this trick. The 'foot tap' would be a very cute addition to a freestyle routine.

Dig. This is our final paw trick. Certain breed have the tendency to be persistent diggers, many terriers in particular. You may be asking yourself "why in the world would I want to teach my dog to dig?!" Most people want dogs to stop digging, not to start. Actually, putting 'dig' on cue and choosing the time and place for it can be helpful. Giving your dog an outlet for the desire to dig may lessen digging at other times. If 'dig' is put on cue, it's a bit less likely to occur if the cue hasn't been given. However, if you have a big digging problem, you may want to skip this trick until you get advice from a trainer. One interesting solution for digging is to provide your dog with a digging pit, and work on directing digging to that specific place. A sand box in which you bury toys and treats would be enticing to your dog, and might keep him away from the rosebushes.

To teach 'dig' as a trick, pick a target for your dog to 'dig' in or on. A large empty dog food bowl would work well for this. You can choose any target that's fairly steady. CT your dog for any interaction with the target. Then narrow your reinforcements to touching the target with his feet. At some point you'll have a dog who's standing with his front feet on the target. Then you'll want to CT foot movement. Natural diggers will pick this up rather quickly, while other dogs may simply shift their feet back and forth on the target. By careful observation, CT faster and faster foot movement.

RETRIEVE TRICKS

Many dogs, even those who are not retrieving breeds, love to retrieve. Others, even retrievers by name, have no desire to put anything other than food in their mouths. Even non-retrievers can learn to pick up and carry objects without stress or force. Free shaping is the best way to accomplish this. Start by choosing a retrieve object. Choose something that will be easy for your dog to pick up and carry. A tennis ball or a short wooden dowel are good choices. Obedience dumbbells come in a number of shapes and sizes. If you decide to use a dumbbell, be sure to have it fitted correctly. The retrieve object is not to chew on or play with. Don't give your dog access to it except during shaping sessions.

If you think about the process of retrieving, you'll notice that there are a large number of steps involved. Your dog must look for the object, move towards it, pick it up, hold it in his mouth, carry it back to you, and release it to you. In obedience competition there are very precise requirements for how each step must be accomplished. In addition, the dog must wait for the signal to retrieve, sit in front of you on the return, and sometimes go over a high jump on the way out to and back from the retrieve object. For this discussion, we'll stick with informal retrieves, although the basic method is the same for obedience retrieves.

Retrieving is a truly useful skill. Dogs can be very helpful by bringing us objects when we ask for them. Service dogs are trained to perform this function for people with physical limitations. As a matter of convenience, it's wonderful to have a dog who will pick up dropped car keys or bring you the telephone. First, I'll talk about the basic method for free shaping a retrieve. Then, I'll talk about applying retrieves to specific uses and tricks.

THE BASIC RETRIEVE

In teaching the retrieve, first think about the individual behaviors/steps the dog must perform. Even a dog who has a fairly strong play retrieve (chasing sticks and balls, for example) needs to go back to the beginning. Don't make any assumptions about what your dog can or should do. Be prepared to progress slowly, step by step. Also, the retrieve is an exercise for which your timing of reinforcement is very important. The click needs to be quick and accurate. Clicking too soon or too late reinforces the wrong thing (more on this in the description of the method).

Begin retrieve training in a distraction free environment. Ideally, your dog already understands the CT connection. You need to be prepared with some special treats. Start by holding the retrieve object in your hand at your dog's face height. Be ready to click any interest your dog shows in the object, even a quick shifting of the eyes in that direction. You may need to move the object around a bit (don't wave it wildly!) Be very observant so that you catch any small movement your dog makes towards the object, or any interest your dog shows.

As your dog starts to understand that the retrieve object is important for CT, responses should start to flow. Remember, have patience. It's best not to lure or 'help' the dog too much. Allow your dog a chance to figure out this new challenge on her own.

An average free shaping session for a retrieve might proceed as the one described below. Remember that your results depend on a number of factors including the setting, your dog, and your shaping abilities.

The twelve basic steps for a retrieve are as follows:

1. Look at the object.
2. Turn head towards the object.
3. Move towards the object.
4. Touch or bump the object.
5. Touch the object with mouth.
6. Open mouth and touch object.
7. Touch the object with teeth.

8. Close teeth over the object.

9. Hold the object in mouth.

10. Turn head towards you while holding the object.

11. Move towards you while holding the object.

12. Drop the object in your hand.

The steps for free shaping a retrieve are roughly as follows:

1. You are holding the retrieve object in your hand. You dog shifts her eyes towards retrieve object. CT.

2. Same.

3. Same.

4. Still holding object. Wait for dog to move head slightly toward the retrieve object. CT.

5. Same.

6. Same.

7. Still holding object. Wait for dog to make a more pronounced head movement towards retrieve object. CT.

8. Same.

9. Same.

10. Still holding object. Wait for dog to move body slightly towards retrieve object. CT.

11. Same.

12. Same.

13. Still holding object. Wait for dog to approach object. CT.

14. Same.

15. Same.

16. Still holding object. Wait for dog to bump or touch object. CT. Etc...

Your dog may get stuck at some point and stop offering behaviors. In a case like this, reinforce an earlier behavior to get the dog working again. Then start moving back up through the steps. If you're lucky, your dog may skip steps, especially if he's already done some retrieving. For example, he might grab the retrieve object out of your hand on the second or third trial. That's fine as long as he performs the skipped steps correctly.

Whenever you click for a desired behavior, expect your dog to drop the retrieve object and come back for her treat. This is fine. The click means "that's it!" but it also means "you're finished for the moment". In working through the steps, you'll be extending the requirements for the retrieve. Dropping the object after a click is expected and acceptable.

Once your dog will reliably take the object from your hand, then give it back, it's time to move the object to different places. Put it on a low table or on the floor. Keep it close to you at first, adding distance as your dog continues to retrieve confidently. Once the dog is reliably retrieving you can start adding a general retrieve cue such as "take it" or "get it". I add cues for specific objects as I teach them.

As I said earlier, timing of the CR is crucial in retrieve shaping. For example, let's say your dog is now touching the retrieve object with his teeth. In trying to raise your criteria, you want to reinforce him for actually taking the object in his mouth. If you click too soon, you're still reinforcing touching with teeth and you'll be stuck at the step. If you click too late you might be reinforcing the dog for removing his teeth from the retrieve object. You need a keen eye to catch the behavior, and quick reflexes to mark the desired behavior. Practice these skills to sharpen them. Offer to train your friend's and neighbor's dogs to retrieve. Go to your local shelter and work with the dogs there. Try to find a training partner who can observe you and offer advice. Remember, learning new skills takes some time and effort, both for you and for your dog. But the results are well worth the effort!

Just because your dog learns a consistent retrieve using a specific object like a dowel rod, that doesn't mean he'll generalize the retrieve to other objects. You need to make an effort to get your dog to pick up a wide range of things. Use objects with various textures, weights, and shapes.

APPLICATIONS OF THE RETRIEVE

Like 'touch', retrieve is also a fundamental skill. It is the basis for many cute and useful behaviors. For those of us who are couch potatoes, putting the dog to work retrieving is a great convenience. Use your imagination in devising retrieve tricks. Some of the following ideas can get you started.

Recycle. For the environmentally-conscious canine. For 'recycle' your dog must take an empty aluminum can and put it into the proper receptacle. Some dogs demonstrate an aversion to taking metal objects in their mouths. You can alter this by regularly feeding them some very tasty food off of a metal spoon. For 'recycle' you will have your dog take the can, go to the proper receptacle, and drop the can into it. These three behaviors make up the 'recycle' chain. As I discussed in chaining earlier, you need to teach each component behavior separately before attempting to put the sequence together. So work on teaching 1) take the can, 2) go to the container, 3) drop the can in the container.

Teach your dog to take the can by presenting the can and giving your retrieve cue. Be generous with your CT at first, then raise your criteria. You want the dog to pick up any can you point out. Once your dog willingly takes the can in her mouth, she needs to go to the recycle container while holding the can. Set up the container so that it's very close at first. Your dog should only have to take one or two steps to reach the container. When she moves towards the container, CT. Gradually increase the number of steps towards the container that your dog must take to earn reinforcement. Your goal is to have your dog go to the usual place where you keep the recycle container while she is still holding the can in her mouth.

Finally, you want to teach your dog to drop the can into the container. Have the container right next to your dog for this. Once you have given her the can to hold make sure her head is directly over the container. Then encourage her to 'drop' or 'out' the can.

You might even hold out your hand, but move it away as your dog releases the can so that it lands in the container. CT when she lets go of the can.

Once your dog can perform each individual part of the exercise, you can start chaining. I would suggest using backchaining for this trick. Start at the end and work forward. Your first step in putting the chain together would be #3, dropping the can into the container. Reinforcement will always come after this step is performed correctly. Once your dog is performing the 'drop' successfully, start adding the middle behavior of going to the container. Increase the distance from the place you give your dog the can to the container. After going to the container, she must drop the can into it before you CT. Once these behaviors are being reliably performed, add the first element: picking up the can. Work on being able to give your dog a can and also directing her to pick one up off of a table. Now all three behaviors must be performed in sequence before you CT. At this point you will also start adding the cue for the entire sequence 'recycle'. Give the 'recycle' cue right before your retrieve cue for the first behavior. At first you'll have to continue giving cues for each part of the chain, but eventually you can fade out all but the first one.

Put away your toys. If you can't always get your kids to perform this behavior, you might have better luck with your dog! Having your dog pick up and put away his toys is a very useful behavior. It will also amaze your friends. To teach this trick, follow the same basic process outlined in describing how to teach 'recycle'. Think about the component parts of the exercise: go to a toy, pick it up, take it to the toy box, drop it into the box. Again, backchaining is a good method for training this sequence. The only difference here is that instead of one specific object (can) you want your dog to pick up all the objects on the floor (toys).

For this trick it helps to teach your dog to take direction while retrieving. You can use a verbal cue and a hand signal to indicate the item that you want your dog to pick up. In competition obedience for the Directed Retrieve exercise (sending your dog to one of three gloves) most people use the word "mark" or "look" along with the left arm extended next to the dog's head and pointing at the object. These cues help your dog to focus on the retrieve object.

If your dog already understands the concept of going towards a target, learning to 'mark' will be fairly easy. Start by setting out a target that's large and easy to see. Go with your dog and have him sit about five feet away, facing the target. Focus your dog on the target by giving the verbal cue and hand signal. CT your dog simply for looking at the target at this stage. After you've practiced 'mark' on a few different objects, you can add the next step, retrieving the object. Set up your dog, give your 'mark' signal, then give your retrieve cue. Keep the distances short in the beginning. As your dog becomes successful at a simple mark and retrieve, you can start asking for multiple behaviors (several mark and retrieves in a row). The eventual number depends on how many toys your dog has.

The middle behavior in this sequence is taking the toy to the toy box, rather than bringing it to you. Start by having the toy box close to you. CT when your dog is near the box with the toy. Slowly start moving the box further and further away from you. You're no longer CTing for a retrieve, but for taking the toy towards the box.

The final behavior is having your dog drop the toy into the toy box. Again, move the box close to you in the early stages of training. Follow the directions above for teaching your dog to drop the can in the recycle container.

Get the phone. Not only an impressive trick, but possibly a life-saver. If I ever break a leg, I definitely want my dog to bring me the phone when I ask. This trick is possible due to the popularity of cordless phones. You might want a practice phone reserved for training this trick. In the beginning, drool and tooth marks are a definite possibility. I take the battery out of the practice phone to make it lighter. Some people use a child's toy phone for this trick rather than a real one.

Introduce your dog to the phone as a retrieve object. Ask for short, quick retrieves at first.

Some phones are heavy and/or hard to carry easily. Give your dog time to get comfortable with the feel of the phone in her mouth. A dog who has already learned to retrieve will start bringing the phone to you fairly quickly.

For entertainment purposes, the best part of this trick is the cue. While a simple "phone" or "get the phone" will work, a dog who retrieves the phone on "ring, ring" (human voice) is sure to get attention. I purposely did not teach a phone retrieve to the real sound of a ringing phone. I don't want to have to race my dogs to get the phone!

Introduce your 'phone' cue by giving it just before you give your all-purpose retrieve cue. With enough pairings, your dog will start to retrieve on the 'phone' cue alone and you can drop the retrieve cue.

Achoo! Also known as the 'sneeze' trick. You sneeze and your dog brings you a tissue so you can wipe your nose. What could be more helpful? I use a handkerchief instead of tissues because my dogs love to shred paper. The handkerchief also holds up to dog saliva better than tissues. However, if you do want to use tissues, you can add the step of having your dog pull the tissue from the box. This is very impressive.

The 'sneeze' trick is taught just like the 'phone' trick. Practice having your dog retrieve the tissue or handkerchief up close. Then add distance to the retrieve. Finally, add your 'sneeze' cue just before your retrieve cue.

Bring the remote. Designed as a labor-saving device, it seems we often spend more time looking for the remote control than we do using it. The remote control loses its convenience when you have to get up and get it. So teach your dog to handle this little chore for you.

As with the phone, I like to train using a practice remote. The remote is not intended as a chew toy, but as a retrieve object. I discourage any mouthing of the remote by taking it away and ignoring the dog for a short time before giving him another opportunity to try the retrieve. This is also a place to use your NRM.

For this trick follow the steps above for teaching the phone and tissue retrieves.

For clumsy owners. There are two things I drop with great regularity: my car keys and my dog's leash. This is probably because I'm always trying to carry too many things at one time. This also means that if I have to bend over and pick the dropped object up, I'll probably drop even more stuff. The easiest solution has been to teach my dogs to pick up these dropped objects and return them to my hand.

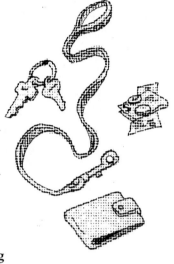

Teach these items as you would any retrieve object. The keys might be more difficult than the leash. Dogs seem to love getting their mouths on their leashes, but would like to avoid metal keys. However, they can learn to pick up both willingly if you use free shaping as your teaching method.

In addition to keys and leashes, your dog can pick up and return just about any dropped item. The larger the variety of objects you practice retrieves on, the easier this task becomes for your dog. I've heard of a Labrador Retriever who picks up dropped change for his owner. Unfortunately, he also swallows it occasionally. So be careful in choosing what you ask your dog to pick up for you.

Bring the biscuit. Personally, I have not been able to teach this to my own dogs. However, I've seen it demonstrated and the method looks easy enough. I believe that most fanatically food-motivated dogs will be unable to resist the temptation. But you may want to give this a try and see for yourself.

For this trick you'll need some large, hard dog biscuits for your dog to retrieve. In order to make this trick work, your PR must be much better than the biscuit. I'd suggest garlic chicken or liver. Start by showing your dog the biscuit. The key is to not allow your dog the opportunity to actually bite into the biscuit at first. Once you've shown your dog the biscuit remove it and CT with your higher value reinforcer. You're reinforcing your dog for noticing the biscuit, but not eating it. With my retrievers, we never get beyond this step. They seem to believe that any food, high value or not, must be eaten immediately.

You'll need to work in very short steps towards getting your dog to take the biscuit in his mouth, but not bite into it. When the biscuit gets soggy, replace it with another one. Don't feed it to your dog! This will send a very confusing message. Always reinforce with your high value treat. I can't think of anything more impressive than a dog who returns the biscuit, uneaten, to the handler. Good luck with this one!

Carry a basket. Choose a basket that is appropriate to your dog's size. It should have a handle on the top that your dog can easily grasp with her mouth. Reinforce your dog for approaching/investigating the basket. Then start reinforcing only for touching the handle. Narrow down your range of acceptable responses to picking up the basket by the handle.

Actually walking while carrying the basket may be a novel idea for your dog. Again, move slowly through the process. CT your dog for standing while holding the basket, then for taking one step, etc.

Basketball. You'll need a small soft basketball and hoop set. These can be purchased at any toy store. Your task here is basically the same as for 'recycle'. You want your dog to pick up the basketball, carry to the hoop, and drop it in. Follow the steps outlined above for 'recycle' to teach these behaviors. You could add a cue phrase such as "slam dunk" for this trick.

Get me a soda/beer. This trick has a number of steps, but is not as difficult as it seems. This is the ultimate in convenience for human couch potatoes! Imagine the luxury of having a dog who can bring you a cold drink from the refrigerator on command. This is another behavior that service dogs are often taught to perform. When broken down into its component parts, you have the following behaviors to train:
1) go to the refrigerator

2) open the refrigerator
3) get a soda
4) bring you the soda
5) close the refrigerator.

You can train #1 (go to the refrigerator) using target training. Start very close to the refrigerator and CT your dog for approaching it. Since most dogs are fascinated by the fridge, this shouldn't be too hard. Follow the steps outlined earlier in the target training session. Use the cue word "refrigerator" or "fridge".

Training #2 (open the refrigerator) is a little different from any tricks discussed so far. You'll need some rope or a towel that can be attached to the refrigerator door handle. First, however, practice tugging with your dog with the rope or towel. When your dog will put some force into pulling, CT. Use the cue word "pull" or "open" for this behavior. Then put the rope or towel on the refrigerator door and encourage your dog to "pull". CT any efforts at first, then ask for pulls that are strong enough to open the door.

To train #3 (get a soda) you need to make sure that your dog clearly understands what the retrieve object is. At this point, you may run into a major problem. Your dog now has access to the food in the refrigerator. You might want to clear everything except soda cans off the bottom shelf so your dog isn't tempted. You'll probably have to use your NRM when your dog decides to investigate the depths of the fridge, then redirect her back to the soda cans. Another possible problem has to do with a dog who has a 'hard' mouth (who grasps things tightly). You may end up with leaky soda cans from this. Encourage your dog to be gentle with the cans. Have some empty practice cans to use at first. When you go to using full cans you may want to wrap a bit of tape around them to give your dog an easy grip and to protect the can.

Once your dog understands #3, training #4 (bring you the soda) should be fairly simple. Stay close by so that you can encourage your dog to bring you the can and then

CT for coming towards you. By now your dog has done enough retrieving to understand that the object in her mouth has a destination. You just need to show her that the destination is you.

Finally, you'll need to teach your dog to perform step #5 (close the refrigerator door). Once your dog has brought you the soda she needs to go back and push the refrigerator door shut with her nose. Again, target training is the easiest way to train this behavior. You might even use a visual target such as a sticker that you put on the refrigerator door where you want your dog to push. Then CT for touching the spot, and eventually shape for harder and harder touches, until your dog will push hard enough to close the door.

You'll need to move further and further away during training so that, eventually, you can give the cues from another room. Lastly, you can put all of the steps together using backchaining.

*I said earlier that this was a great trick for human couch potatoes. However, if you've gone to the trouble of teaching this trick, you're probably not a couch potato at all!

MISCELLANEOUS TRICKS

The following tricks don't necessarily fit into a specific category, but they are some common favorites.

Kiss. It's hard to imagine, but some people find dog saliva disgusting. On the other hand, many of us find a dog's kiss to be a rather endearing thing. Before you start, be sure you have a dog who will 'kiss' gently. Dogs who are very energetic and excitable may not be capable of performing this trick safely.

A quick and easy way to teach 'kiss' is to hold a piece of food between your lips and encourage your dog to take the food gently, clicking when she touches the food/your lips. At first, hold your face close to your dog's and have her watch as you place the food between your lips. As your dog starts to understand the behavior you can fade the food lure and point to your lips (using the same hand motion you used to place food there).

Some dogs may respond to a 'kissing sound' by moving towards the source (your mouth). You could then CT for this behavior.

Speak. Teaching your dog to vocalize can be a very useful behavior. A dog who will bark on cue can give you a great feeling of security. However, many dogs enjoy 'speak' just a little too much. Therefore, we'll discuss how to teach 'quiet' shortly.

You'll need to find some way to encourage your dog to make noise so that you can CT that behavior. You might have a dog who you know will bark at certain stimuli (the mail being delivered, the neighbor's dog). If you CT when your dog barks at this, you will reinforce barking. Unfortunately, you may be reinforcing inappropriate barking. It would be better if you could elicit barking in a different context.

One way to encourage your dog to make sounds is to expose her to a mild stressor. One very effective way to do this is to slightly delay delivery of your dog's meals. Prepare your dog's food bowl and have your clicker ready. Stand with the full food bowl in your hands and wait. Your dog may try a variety of behaviors, but most dogs eventually make some noise, even a slight whine. CT any sound your dog makes, using a piece of kibble as your PR. Over a number of trials you can shape this whine into louder and louder vocalizations. You might even give a 'jackpot' (a very large, unexpected reinforcer) for a good 'speak' by simply setting down the food bowl for your dog. Jackpots are very effective motivators. They make a huge impression.

Talk. Once your dog has learned to 'speak' you can discriminate between different types of vocalizations. 'Talk' is simply a quieter version of 'speak'. You can shape 'talk' by reinforcing only the quieter attempts to 'speak'. Some dogs can manage a very interesting and humorous tone.

Quiet. For some people, teaching 'quiet' is much more important than teaching 'speak'. Certain breeds, particularly herding dogs, seem predisposed to barkiness. 'Quiet' can be taught in a positive, rather than a negative, manner.

Be prepared to CT 'quiet' immediately after barking. If you know that certain things will trigger barking, then you can be ready. After several barks you need to get your dog's attention back to you. At first you literally might have to wave a treat right under your dog's nose. If you can get your dog to interrupt his barking even momentarily, CT for the quiet. Timing is very important here. You have to be able to catch the dog being quiet, rather than barking. You don't want to unintentionally reinforce the barking, thereby increasing rather than decreasing it.

If your dog gets too focused/excited and won't take food while barking, you need to find something else to get his attention. Playing with a favorite squeaky toy or opening the refrigerator might work. Anything that interrupts the barking and gets a moment of quiet is all you need. Then you can CT.

If your dog has a good recall you might be able to call your dog away from the 'bark stimulus'. Then you can CT for the quiet that occurs as the dog turns/moves towards you.

Yawn. You can probably get an approximation of a yawn rather than a genuine one. Start working on this behavior by CTing anytime your dog opens her mouth. Over time slowly shape for bigger and bigger mouth movements.

Getting the real thing on cue is possible, but more difficult. You'll need to be prepared to reinforce when your dog yawns on her own. Many dogs yawn at predictable times, such as when they wake up from a nap. If you're ready and can catch this a few times, your dog may start to get the idea. There are two great cues for this. One is to yawn first yourself, then have your dog yawn as if in response. The other is to ask the dog "are you tired?"

Head on knee. This is a very cute behavior. Your dog puts his head on your knee and looks up at you lovingly. However, you may end up with a dog who drools on your leg! If your dog has already learned to put her 'head down' on the floor, you should find it fairly easy to move this behavior to another target (your knee). You can train this using a target stick and placing it on your leg. Most dogs can pick up on this quite quickly.

Another method would be to free shape the behavior. At first CT anytime your dog's head is close to your leg. Then raise your expectations and only CT for your dog having his head next to your leg, then actually on your leg, then in one specific place on your leg.

Get your tail. A number of dogs chase their tails. Most humans find this quite amusing. I'm not sure why either of these things are true. In any case, we can teach tail chasing if it's not a natural behavior, or simply put it on cue if it is. Of course, this could be quite a challenge for dogs without tails or with very short or upright ones. However, you could still teach this behavior as a variation of 'spin'.

If you have a natural tail-chaser, you simply need to be ready to CT when the behavior occurs. If not, you might train this trick by teaching your dog to target her tail. For dogs with longer tails, you can gently pull the tail around to the dog's side and wiggle it. Then CT when she pays attention to the tail.

You could also use a target stick and move it further and further around towards your dog's tail while asking for and reinforcing 'touch'.

Dogs who chase their tails are cute, but dogs who actually catch them are quite impressive! You need a long-tailed, flexible dog for this trick. Long hair on the tail is a plus because it's easy for your dog to grab and hold. Once your dog is reliably tail-chasing, start reinforcing only for closer and closer 'catches'. Of course, once they catch their tails, they never seem to know quite what to do with them.

I use both a verbal cue and a hand signal for tail-chasing. I stand facing Sully, put both hands out at my sides, palms up, and ask "where's your tail?" First he looks to one side, then the other, then starts spinning until he catches it. It doesn't exactly make him look like a canine Einstein, but it's a pretty cute trick anyway.

Find it. This trick is a good way to start teaching your dog to use her nose as well as her eyes to find things. First, pick a toy that your dog already plays with often and is willing to retrieve to use as your 'find' object. I use a Kong™ toy for this because of its distinctive shape and size. Have your dog 'sit' and 'wait'. Show your dog the toy, allowing her to sniff it as well as see it. Use an excited and enthusiastic tone and manner to motivate her. Place the toy on the floor about five feet in front of your dog and encourage her to 'find it'. This should be easy for your dog. As soon as she reaches down to sniff or pick up the toy, CT. If your dog is already a good retriever, you can ask her to bring the toy back to you. If not, work on retrieves separately before adding them to the game.

Once your dog understands the concept of 'finding' her toy when it's in plain sight, you can start making the game more challenging. Put the toy under a blanket or pillow while your dog watches. Have your dog wait while you place the toy just around a corner. Make the hiding places progressively harder. Hide the toy on a dining room chair or in the bathtub. When the toy is no longer in plain sight your dog will have to start relying on her sense of smell to 'find it'.

I make this trick a competition between my dogs. They both must 'sit' and 'wait' while I hide the toy in another room. Then I release them to go 'find it'. The winner is very proud of his/her accomplishment and loves parading around with the prize. This is a good rainy day activity to burn off some energy.

Instead of finding an object, you can teach your dog to search for and find different people. This is a great game for kids to play with the dog. Start with the 'find object' in plain sight. Have the child call the dog for CT. Then have the child (to be found) go around the corner and call while the person in the room encourages the dog to 'find him'. As with the toy, make this progressively harder. Eventually you can have the child hide under a bed or in a closet and the dog will search for him. Whenever the dog finds the child he gets CTd. If a dog is having trouble with a 'find' the person can help by calling the dog softly.

With enough consistency and repetition your dog can even learn the names of different family members and be sent to find a specific person. For example, "find Chris" or "find Robin" can be used as cues just before that person calls the dog

.

You never know, some day this trick could be a true lifesaver.

Get .... Dogs can learn the names of many objects. They can be taught to discriminate between different toys and bring a specific one. The keys to teaching this are consistency and repetition. Start with a single toy. Show your dog the toy and repeat its name several times. Sully has a stuffed bear with black spots that we call (creatively) "Spot". I started teaching the name for this toy by showing it to Sully and excitedly saying "look, here's SPOT", "see SPOT?", "where's SPOT?" Then I threw Spot a short distance and encouraged Sully to retrieve him for CT. Once Sully would retrieve Spot reliably I'd make it harder. Next I would quietly place Spot on the floor when Sully wasn't paying attention and start asking "where's SPOT?", "bring me SPOT", "can you find SPOT?" Any movement in Spot's direction led to CT. Again, I waited for a reliable response to this before moving on. Finally, I would ask Sully to choose Spot from 2-3 toys on the floor, CTing for correct choices.

You can repeat this process for any number of different toys. When you're in the teaching stages keep it simple for your dog. Make it easy for him to be right. Make sure that the correct choice is obvious. Don't ask your dog to discriminate between different toys until he's learned the individual names and can reliably bring you the requested object.

Once you're certain that your dog has learned the names of individual toys, you can start asking him to make some simple discriminations. Start with two obviously different toys (such as a stuffed toy and a bone). Have the toys spaced well apart (at least ten feet) and turn your dog in the direction of the one you are requesting. Anything you can do to increase your dog's chance for success is helpful. CT your dog when you're absolutely sure he's choosing the correct object. Once he can distinguish between two objects you can add more. When adding and switching items you might find that your dog keeps returning to the first object you taught. Have patience. Simply quit reinforcing that object for a while and try to find ways to make it an easier exercise for your dog.

You can make this a useful trick by teaching your dog to pick up your shoes, books, the kids' toys, etc. You need to follow the same teaching process for each new item.

PRESENTATION AND COSTUMES

Set-ups. If you're going to show off your dog's skills, you need to think a bit about how you set-up and present the behavior. This can make all the difference between a cute trick and a truly impressive one. A little bit of dramatic flair can be a wonderful way to showcase your dog's talents. Once you've gone to all the work of training the behaviors, you want to present them for the best effect possible.

Your explanation or description prior to the trick, along with the cue, creates an expectation in the audience. There are some very creative, amusing ways to set-up and present even the most simple behaviors so that they seem more interesting and difficult.

I knew a woman with a Dalmatian who used her dog's behaviors to discuss fire safety with children. She taught her dog to stop (stand/stay), drop (down), and roll (roll over) to show kids what to do in case of fire. For added dramatic effect she taught her dog to crawl to her (out of a burning building) after the roll. These children would certainly remember the behaviors this dog demonstrated.

Another woman had a Poodle who she had taught to do a retrieve. This is usually a fairly simple behavior to teach. To make it more interesting she placed three stuffed animals along the dog's path. The animals were a lion, a tiger, and a bear. Then she explained how her dog was frightened of wild animals, but she had learned to be brave and pass the 'lions and tigers and bears' to complete her retrieve.

I taught my Lab, Katie, to twist between my legs in a figure 8 pattern. One day I presented this as "Katie's kitty cat imitation". The response was much better than when it was simply a figure 8.

Rather than simply asking Sully to 'speak' I cue him to bark rather enthusiastically by asking him "are you a guard dog?" This works because he's a goofy Golden Retriever and obviously not very tough. It would be even more effective with a small, fluffy dog.

Instead of asking for a 'kiss' you can cue the dog with the question "who do you love?" This one's sure to get ooohhhs and aaahhhs.

I knew a guy who used the cue "Rambo" to get his dog to crawl. You could just picture him crawling under barbed wire in the jungle. Something as simple as changing a 'down' cue to 'bang!' can be very effective.

With a little bit of thought you can probably come up with some unique ways of presenting behaviors. Have fun with it and be creative.

Costumes. The use of costumes can be lots of fun. Remember dressing up the family pets when you were a kid? Some pets were very mellow and laid-back about the whole ordeal, while others literally fought tooth and nail.

Even dogs who are initially less than thrilled with the idea of dressing up can learn to tolerate costumes. The key to teaching this tolerance is desensitization. Desensitization simply means slowly getting the animal used to the stimulus. Desensitization is used in humans to help cure unrealistic fears and phobias. A good program of desensitization needs a little forethought and planning. The most important thing to remember is to only proceed to the next step when the dog is completely comfortable. The following example describes a typical desensitization process.

Last Halloween I bought an 'angel' outfit for Sully. Those who know him would see the irony in this. The outfit had a halo on a headband and a set of glittery wings with elastic to hold them in place. Sully is not the calmest or most temperamentally stable of dogs, and, at first, just the sight of this costume sent him running into the next room. However, he did learn to be comfortable wearing the costume in time for the Halloween party.

You start desensitizing at the place at which your dog is comfortable. I started with Sully by putting the costume in the middle of the kitchen table, then sitting on a chair with clicker and treats. Sully was willing to come to me for CT. At first he eyed the costume suspiciously, probably wondering "does it eat Golden Retrievers?" But he quickly started ignoring it as he was much more interested in treats. Then I moved the costume to the edge of the table, next to me. This caused him a bit of concern, he jumped back, then cautiously approached again. I continued to CT him simply for approaching me. Once he was again ignoring the costume, I moved it to my lap. He displayed the same avoidance then approach pattern. Once he was calm at that step, I held the wings in one hand at my side. Once he was approaching easily I moved on to the next step, moving the wings toward him. These small steps continued until I could hold the wings on his back. The next step was to loop the elastic over his legs. Once that was accomplished I worked on increasing the time he wore the wings. Finally, he had to learn that he could walk while wearing the wings.

All of these steps occurred a number of short training sessions. In all, it took about a week. It probably would have gone faster if I had done more short sessions per day. As with free shaping, you need to lower your criteria or raise it depending on your dog's behavior. Don't push to get this done in a specific time frame. The most important factor for success is always allowing your dog the option of leaving if he is uncomfortable. If he's motivated by your PR, he'll choose to return. Trying to force a dog, or moving through the steps too fast, will only make your dog's reluctance even stronger.

During this entire process keep your talking to a minimum. Don't try to coax or calm your dog with your voice. Often, this only makes the problem worse. Instead, rely on the power of CT training.

Always think of your dog's comfort and safety when picking out costumes. Avoid anything with small parts that your dog might swallow. Be careful of sharp or rough edges. Some materials can be itchy.

When buying ready-made costumes simple alterations can make them much easier for your dog to wear. Many human costumes can be adapted for dogs. Adding elastic can make some costumes fit much better. For example, costumes with headbands can benefit from sewing on a piece of elastic to hold them under your dog's chin. If you have any sewing abilities, you may want to try making your own costumes. You can be as creative as you want.

When choosing costumes, consider your dog's personality and the type of trick or the event for which it will be worn. Something as simple as a scarf to match the season or holiday can add to your dog's appeal. One of my dogs is certified by the Delta society as a therapy dog. When we visit hospitals and nursing homes I often add a scarf or a simple costume. This seems to make her look less intimidating and more approachable. A dog wearing bunny ears is certainly not going to scare anyone!

Sometimes the best costume is no costume at all. My friend has a beautiful Rough Collie named Rhin. One Halloween Rhin was at the door as she was giving out candy. A little girl exclaimed to her mother "Look, her dog has a 'Lassie' costume!"

4 *Games*

CHAPTER 4: GAMES

Games can be lots of fun as well as a great way to learn. The beauty of games is that they often make work seem like play. I like to use lots of games in my classes. They help people and dogs relax. They're a great way to get students to interact with each other and their dogs. People seem quite motivated to work on behaviors that may lead to winning a game. There's also a lot of pride in doing well in a game, even a silly one.

A word of warning about games and competition is in order. Some people get very intense during competition. You might be surprised by how important winning becomes. If you use games in your classes, be careful that no one takes them too seriously. It's a good idea to have some sort of prize for everyone, including a 'best sport' or 'best effort' prize. I usually have dog treats for everyone, and a couple small toys as special prizes. In addition, I make a real effort to comment favorably on something about each dog/handler team during the game. Your attitude can go a long way towards keeping the atmosphere light and fun.

Many of the games I describe can be played either as individual or group games. You can use them in your own training, try them when training with friends, or add them to your classes. Games are always a big hit!

Puppy push-ups. We start these in puppy classes. A puppy push-up is simply a 'sit then down' sequence. The goal is to see how many you can do in 30 seconds. For puppy and beginner classes, you can let your students use a food lure. For more advanced classes, you can specify either voice only or hand signal only for the cue. You can also do 'stand then down' push-ups for more difficulty.

Recall games. There are a number of games that can help make recall practice fun. Since some of these are exciting, active games, be sure that the dogs who play them are reliable off-lead and very dog-friendly.

Recall game #1: Time recalls of equal distance. Give a prize for fastest recall, but also a 'prize' for slowest recall as well. Try to do a slow recall on purpose, it's not necessarily easy.

Recall game #2: Have a recall relay with teams. Equal numbers of dogs and handlers will be on each team. Each team goes separately. Handlers leave their dogs in a line on a 'stay'. Time starts when the first handler calls his or her dog. Once the dog reaches his handler, the second handler calls. Dogs must 'sit/stay' in front of handlers until the relay is completed. Time ends when the last dog reaches his handler. Any dog who moves from in front of his handler incurs a 2-second penalty.

Recall game #3: This is more of a distraction exercise than a competitive game. But it's still fun! This game is for handlers with more advanced dogs. Have two handlers leave their dogs on the same side of the room, but at opposite ends. The handlers leave their dogs and walk to the opposite corner of the room, crossing each other in the middle.

Handlers take turns calling their dogs. Any dog who leaves position before being called is returned and reminded to 'stay'. You can make this more difficult by adding other dogs and handlers at random positions. Vary the time dogs must 'stay' before being called. Occasionally, have a handler return to the dog and release him. You can also scatter toys and objects on the floor as distractions. However, make sure the dogs are ready for this level of proofing. Don't set them up for failure. Make it possible for them to be successful by increasing difficulty slowly over time.

Recall game #4: This is a game to play at home with your dog. Do random recalls from one room to another. Make a big deal of the successful recall. Gradually make it harder and harder for your dog to find you. Hide under the kitchen table. Hide in a closet. Hide in the shower stall. When your dog finds you, have a party! Roll on the floor, play silly games, pull out a special toy or treat. These random recalls will greatly increase the reliability of the behavior.

Crazy dog game. This game involves playing with your dog in any way you want in an effort to get him revved up and excited. Then give a cue for 'sit' or 'down'. Once you give the cue stop playing, stand up straight, and wait for your dog to comply. As soon as the dog obeys, go back to playing again. To make this game more difficult you can require the dog to hold the position for longer and longer periods before going back to play. You can also add some harder positions, such as 'stand' and 'finish'.

Ball in a hoop. This one requires a couple of pieces of equipment. You'll need a large ball, such as a Boomer ball, and a hula hoop. Put the hula hoop flat on the floor and put the ball in the middle of it. The purpose of the game is for the dog to push the ball out of the hoop. The handler cannot touch the dog, ball, or hoop. She also cannot bend over the hoop. Verbal signals and encouragements are the only techniques the handler can use. For some 'ball crazy' dogs this is a very easy task. For others, it can be quite difficult.

> Hint: If a dog knows 'touch' then this is a fairly simple exercise. Just apply 'touch' to the ball and reinforce harder and harder touches, until the dog pushes the ball.

Retrieve races. You can set up retrieve races with a number of variations. When more than one dog is retrieving at the same time, be very sure that they are dog-friendly.

Retrieve race #1: Two handlers place a retrieve object equal distances from themselves and their dogs. They return to their dogs and send them at the same time. The first dog to retrieve his own retrieve object wins. You can run this game in heats, with the winner going on to the next challenger.

Retrieve race #2: A number of retrieve objects are placed in a chalk-drawn square. The handler has one minute to have the dog retrieve as many objects as possible. The handler must not move his feet and the dog must deliver each object to hand.

Retrieve race #3: The handler repeatedly throws the same retrieve object for the dog. The number of retrieves completed in one minute are counted. Again, the handler must not move his feet and the dog must deliver the object to hand.

Retrieve race #4: This is a relay race. A team of dogs and handlers stands in a line. The first handler throws her retrieve object. Once that retrieve is complete and the dog has returned to heel position the next handler throws her retrieve object. There is a minimum distance, marked by a chalk line, for the throws. Teams are timed and the quickest time wins.

Retrieve race #5: Put out a number of different retrieve objects, but designate only certain ones as 'correct'. Dogs earn points for retrieving 'correct' objects, but lose points for retrieving 'incorrect' ones. Handlers must stand at a designated distance from the objects. Hand and verbal signals are acceptable. Number of points earned in one minute are added.

Retrieve race #6: The retrieve objects in this game are large plastic Easter eggs. Be careful that the dogs in this game will not crack or chew on the eggs. The small pieces could be dangerous. Notes describing prizes are inside each egg. You can give prizes such as dog biscuits, candy, dog toys, class discounts, etc. The eggs are all placed in a circle 8 feet away from the dog and handler. The dog is sent to retrieve. The dog/handler team wins the prize in the egg the dog brings back (if the dog brings one back!) The dog must return the egg directly to the handler, who cannot move out of position.

Dumbbell toss. This is related to the retrieve games, but is just for handlers. Set up a target for dumbbell throws. You can use a hula hoop or a chalk circle. You might even draw in a bull's eye. The handler who makes the largest number of accurate tosses wins. This is a great game to improve throwing skills. Make this harder by putting a high jump between the handler and the target. Keep adding boards to make the jump higher.

Changing contexts. I first encountered this idea at an Ian Dunbar seminar. The exercise involves asking for simple behaviors, but making them more difficult by changing some of the cues and contexts. For example, sit in a chair with your back to your dog and ask for a 'sit'. Or lie on the floor and give a 'down' cue. You could stand facing away from your dog and give a 'come' command. You could even try giving commands from out of sight. Dogs who can respond even when the context has changed show true understanding.

Top this. Now your trick training can come into play. In 'top this' two handlers and dogs compete to see who can keep thinking up different behaviors. Each team has thirty seconds to perform a behavior that hasn't been performed by either team. Any behavior is acceptable. One team is out when they can't think of a new behavior in the designated time or when the dog refuses to respond. For example, team 1 does a 'sit', team 2 does a 'down', team 1 does a 'stand', team 2 does a 'bow', etc. until one team fails to perform a unique behavior. If you've trained a number of tricks, you and your dog will be hard to beat on this one.

Round robin. This game requires a group of dog/handler teams. As with 'top this' each team must perform a unique behavior in a specified time. However, each team must also repeat, in order, the behaviors of the other teams. This game starts out easy, but becomes difficult very quickly. Coming up with a unique behavior is hard enough, but having to remember everything that came before is extremely challenging. Those who make mistakes or fail to perform a new behavior drop out of the group until only one person is left.

Tic/tac/drop. This is a well-known favorite of many class instructors. It requires that the dogs be able to perform a moving drop. Dogs must also be able to 'down/stay' despite heavy distractions. Most importantly, they must be comfortable with other dogs moving around and over them.

Use masking tape or chalk to draw a large tic/tac/toe grid on the floor. Make sure each square is larger than the largest dog in the group. One team of dogs and handlers is designated as Xs and the other as Os. Handlers leave their dogs behind a line on one side of the grid, go to the other side, then call their dogs and signal them to drop in a square. If a dog drops between two squares, the square in which more of the dog landed is the one that counts. The goal is for a team to get 3 dogs in a row of squares. If a dog 'breaks' (gets up after he has dropped) that dog leaves the grid and gets another turn at the end.

An easier variation of this game is 'sits and downs' rather than Xs and Os. One team does 'sits' and the other 'downs'. In this variation handlers are allowed to place their dogs in a square and give a stay command. First one dog and handler from a team goes, then one from the other team. Toss a coin, or have a team member guess a number, to decide who goes first. The first team to have their dogs all sitting or lying down in a row wins. If a dog 'breaks' he is taken out of the grid and gets another turn at the end of the game. Then reverse the 'sits and downs' designations and play again.

Attention. In the attention game, the goal is to hold the dog's attention for as long as possible. In the easiest version of this game the handler can do anything except touch the dog in order to keep her attention. To make it more difficult you can forbid the use of toys, food, or verbal encouragement. This game can be played in heats with two handlers and dogs competing. The first dog to look away is out, and another challenger comes in.

Last one out. The purpose of this game is to perform the largest number of behaviors without reinforcement. This game is played with a group of dogs and handlers listening to an instructor call commands (sit, down, stand, finish, etc.) Handlers can use only verbal reinforcement. The instructor allows ten seconds between commands. Any dog who is not in the correct position when the next command is called is 'out'. The last dog/handler team left is the winner.

*A dog who is 'out' should be taken aside, given a well-learned cue, and generously reinforced. We don't want to extinguish behavior, just see how persistent it is.

'Catch me' game. This is a way to teach dogs to catch up and maintain heel position. The handler and dog are alone in the ring with the dog off-lead. The handler has a clicker and a wonderful primary reinforcer. The handler starts with the dog sitting in heel position and reinforces the dog generously. Then the handler starts walking around the ring briskly in a large left circle. Whenever the dog is in perfect heel position the handler CTs. There are no commands in this game. The dog needs to figure out that heel position is that magic place where reinforcement occurs. Handlers should be prepared to keep walking even when the dog is sniffing or wandering around without them. Eventually, all dogs approach their handlers. You might have to shape a good heel position by reinforcing any movement on the handler's left side, then getting more demanding in your expectations. A dog who maintains heel position should get generous CT at first (every 3-4 steps), then increase required time in heel position.

There are variations on the 'catch me' game that give practice in clicker training skills. At first, you could make the game easier for handlers by having the instructor or an assistant click at the right moment. Then the handler treats. It's often easier for someone observing to see proper heel position than it is for the handler. This will help handlers get a good picture of heel position from their perspective.

You can then have your students become the 'clicker' for each other. Have teams in which one works her dog and gives the treats when the other clicks. This builds observational skills in the student doing the clicking.

Egg races. Play this game using plastic spoons and plastic Easter eggs that open. Inside the eggs put notes describing prizes. The prizes can be things such as dog biscuits, dog calendars or posters, key chains, a discount on class fees, human candy, etc. Players randomly choose their eggs from a basket and are not allowed to open them to look at their prizes.

Students should put the egg on the spoon and hold them in the same hand as their leashes. They must then complete a specified course without dropping the egg. If they do this, they can keep the prize noted inside. If not, they lose the prize. You can make this a timed race between teams or individuals, with only those with the quickest times getting to keep the prizes. Or you could devise an obstacle course consisting of weaving around chairs or traffic cones, walking over low jumps or bars placed on the floor, and passing other dogs and people. You can make the obstacle course as easy or as difficult as your class can handle. Another variation for a competition class would be to call a standard heeling pattern including halts, changes of pace, and turns. The dog/handler team who keeps their egg the longest wins.

Doggie decathlon. The doggie decathlon is a wonderful graduation night activity for your classes. It can be flexible; the actual events will depend on the class level. The decathlon is a team activity made up of ten events. Each team can decide which members will perform each exercise. Unless specifically stated, only one dog and handler needs to perform each of the events. However, each team member must perform at least one exercise. I evaluate teams on both performance and style. Style is quite subjective and can include points for 'cuteness' if you like.

Team members must pass an object (similar to a baton in a relay race) between them during the decathlon. The handler who is working at the moment must have the object. I use a chew bone, but any dog toy would do. The competing team can assess a point penalty if they notice that the working handler doesn't have the object.

I give each handler a sheet listing the events and the rules and go over it in detail. Teams are formed in a random manner. It's often a good idea to have a team captain. Someone needs to be responsible for making quick decisions. Then I allow about twenty minutes for teams to familiarize themselves with the rules and exercises, plan their strategies, and practice.

The following is an example of a doggie decathlon for a class with a wide range of abilities. Since each dog and handler only has to perform a few of the exercises, you can vary the difficulty level.

DOGGIE DECATHLON

The Doggie Decathlon is a set of ten individual exercises. Each team will decide which members will perform each exercise. Each team member must perform at least one exercise. Teams will be evaluated on performance and style.

The team member who is working must have possession of the chew bone. You will incur a penalty if any member of the other team notices that you do not have the chew bone.

*You will have some time to plan your strategy and practice prior to the decathlon.

THE TEN EVENTS

1. **The popcorn toss.** Have your dog do a sit/stay in the chalk circle on the floor. You must move away from your dog behind the chalk line (about 6 feet). Your dog must catch 3 pieces of popcorn without leaving the circle.

2. **Hand signals.** Have your dog stand in the chalk circle on the floor. You may stay as close as you like. However, you can earn double points if you go at least 6 feet away. Using only hand signals instruct your dog to sit, down, and stand.

3. **Voice control.** Have your dog stand in the chalk circle on the floor. You may stay as close as you like. However, you can earn double points if you go at least 6 feet away. Using only voice commands instruct your dog to sit, down, and come.

4. **Retrieve.** Your dog must retrieve an object thrown at least 6 feet and return it to your hand. You may not move your feet during this exercise.

5. Recall over 2 jumps. (Set the jumps low, 8-12 inches). Have your dog do a 'sit/stay' about 8 feet in front of the jumps. You will go the other side of the second jump. Call your dog. Your dog must complete both jumps and sit in front of you.

6. Trick. You and your dog can complete any trick you would like. No food or lures may be used.

7. Puppy push-ups. This is the exercise that all team members must complete. Each member, in sequence, must do 5 puppy push-ups (sit/down/sit/down...) You can use lures or food if necessary. At least one team member must do stand/down push-ups.

8. Agility. You must send your dog through the tunnel to the pause table. Do a 10-second down on the table (another team member should count for you 1,001, 1,002, 1,003...) If your dog breaks the down the counting must start over.

9. Sit/stay. Have your dog 'sit/stay' in the chalk circle on the floor. Go at least 6 feet away and do 5 jumping jacks. Return to heel position and release your dog. If your dog breaks you must start all over.

10. Ball in a hoop. (Described in more detail on page 76). You dog must push the ball out of the hula hoop. You can use verbal instructions and encouragement only. You may not touch the dog, ball, or hoop. You may not lean over the hoop.

EVALUATION OF THE DOGGIE DECATHLON

Each exercise will be worth 5 points (50 points total). All 5 points will be awarded if the exercise is performed as described. In addition, extra points may be added for the style in which the exercise is performed. Energy, intensity, and cuteness count!

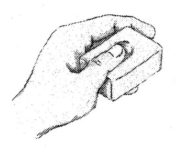

5 *Lesson Plans*

CHAPTER 5: LESSON PLANS FOR A 4-WEEK CLICKS & TRICKS CLASS

A Clicks & Tricks class is a great way to introduce people to clicker training. Most students find it an enjoyable way to interact with their dogs. This is an especially good class for those who are already familiar with more traditional methods of dog training. It offers an interesting and non-threatening alternative to force-based methods.

These lesson plans are meant to be a flexible guide. Once you impart the basic information, change or alter exercises to suit your needs and the interests of your class.

After the first four weeks of class you might want to continue the same basic format in a Fun & Games class. A Fun & Games class can incorporate more advanced trick training, team and group games, and beginning agility (tunnel, pause table, weave poles, jumping, contact zones, sendaways, etc.)

Instructor's Guides. In designing the instructor's guides, I assume that the user is familiar with basic operant conditioning concepts and the use of the clicker. For me, the instructor guides are visual reminders of the ideas I want to present. I always keep an instructor's guide handy to refer to during classes. This keeps me from skipping important information.

Classes are meant to run about an hour, but will vary depending on the number of students you have, and the complexity of your explanations.

Homework Sheets. These homework sheets are designed to give your students guidelines for practice between classes. They repeat key information and remind students of the basic ideas presented in class.

WEEK 1 INSTRUCTOR'S GUIDE

1. Have students sit in chairs spaced as widely apart as practical. Have them sit, or put a foot on, their leashes. Dogs should have enough leash to sit, stand, or lay down.

2. Introduce the purpose of the class. Talk about operant conditioning (in very basic terms), clickers, and the proper use of food in training.

3. Demonstrate clicker conditioning with an untrained dog. Make sure students understand the reason and the mechanics. Point out that the treat must immediately follow the click, so treats must be easily accessible. Discuss options if the dog seems afraid of the clicker (muffle the click, click while the dog is eating, choose a different conditioned reinforcer, etc.)

4. Hand out clickers and have students begin conditioning. They can move out around the training area if they need more room. Instruct them to click & treat (CT) about twenty times. Don't talk or give any commands to the dog during conditioning.

5. Address any questions or problems before continuing.

6. Have students return to their chairs. Tell them to only CT when the dog sits or lays down. Again, no commands, just keep an eye on the dog and reinforce the desired behavior.

7. While students are reinforcing sits or downs, talk about free shaping. Explain what free shaping is and why we do it. Explain the basics of how it's done. If you have a click-wise dog you can demonstrate, but keep it short and simple. Video of a shaping session would be a good addition at this point.

8. Talk about the different ways dogs might react to free shaping. Some dogs 'freeze' and offer very little behavior. Others 'throw' lots of behaviors so it's hard to catch a specific one. Talk about the behaviors you might shape: turning head, twitching ears, moving feet,

wagging tail, etc. Talk about choosing a natural behavior and refining it.

9. Demonstrate free shaping with a student's dog. Choose wisely. Look for an active, outgoing dog. Again, don't go on for too long, just long enough for students to get the idea. You might introduce "101 things to do with a box" here.

10. Have students move out around the training area and stand on their leashes, leaving plenty of slack. Have them start free shaping for any behavior other than a sit or down. Emphasize picking up on very small behaviors; not waiting for a finished product. Help people individually during this exercise. Spend about ten minutes on this.

11. Have students return to their chairs while you talk about refining behaviors by raising and lowering criteria for reinforcement. Talk about working towards a target behavior by slowly asking for more and more extreme versions of the behavior.

12. Answer any questions.

13. Show a target stick, give a very quick explanation, and tell everyone to bring one for next week's class.

14. Hand out homework sheets.

WEEK 1 HOMEWORK SHEET

Welcome to Clicks & Tricks class! There are two goals for this class: learning about clicker training and learning how to teach your dog tricks. Both of these things should be fun for you and your dog.

Please approach this class with an open mind and a willingness to experiment with new and different techniques. Some of the methods may seem strange or unusual at first, but they do work.

The training methods we will be using are based on a scientific learning theory known as operant conditioning (OC). Most trainers already use OC, so you may be familiar with many of the ideas. We will focus on positive reinforcement for desired behaviors.

WHY CLICKS & WHY TREATS?

This class will introduce you to the proper way to use a clicker as a conditioned (learned) reinforcer. A clicker can be a very useful tool for telling your dog "That's it! You did the right thing!" A clicker is used to 'catch' or 'mark' the exact behavior we like. A click is faster than a word, easy to hear even in a noisy environment, and unusual. The click also gives us a moment before we present the primary reinforcer (food).

We typically use food as the primary reinforcer because it's readily available, desirable to most dogs, and quickly consumable. Most dogs will work (often very enthusiastically) to obtain food. We will make the connection between the click and food by repeatedly pairing the click and the treat. Always click first and offer the treat as soon as possible afterwards. Do not click without treating! The click then treat (CT) process is called clicker conditioning. You're teaching your dog that the click is a signal that food is forthcoming. Repeat the click and treat process at least twenty times a day for the first week.

LEARNING THE RULES OF THE TRAINING GAME: PURE SHAPING

Both you and your dog will need to learn how this new type of training game works. Many training methods rely on physically manipulating the dog into the position you would like. In shaping, we let the dog decide what to do. We reinforce those behaviors that we like and ignore those we don't like. Over time the reinforced behaviors will increase and the ignored ones will decrease.

In the first learning stages in shaping we allow the dog to make behavioral choices. Whenever the dog's behavior coincides with what we would like to see, we reinforce it. We don't punish, or even acknowledge wrong behaviors at first. Your dog is learning an important lesson here: that her actions can lead to a pleasant consequence. She is learning how to work the human hot dog dispenser (you).

SHAPING A SPONTANEOUS (EMITTED) BEHAVIOR

This week your goal is to shape a behavior that your dog naturally performs. Start with some small behavior and selectively reinforce the dog for that. As the dog catches on we require more and more precision in the behavior. Watch for something your dog does naturally that you think is cute and CT that. If you can't think of anything else, you could work on reinforcing your dog for turning her head to the left or the right. You might simply decide to reinforce the first behavior you see (scratching, ear twitching, tail wagging, etc.)

SHAPING TIPS

1. Gather your treats, clicker, and dog.

2. Be quiet during shaping. Try not to talk at all.

3. Don't touch your dog or try to help her move into position. In shaping, your dog must freely emit the behavior. If your dog sits and stares at you and does nothing, move around a bit and reinforce her for any movement.

4. Maintain a pleasant facial expression. Smile at your dog. Relax.

5. Watch your dog closely for any movement. You must be very observant.

6. Start by reinforcing any slight movement in the direction you desire. You can tell that your dog 'gets it' if she starts repeating the behavior over and over.

7. Once your dog is repeating the behavior, start waiting for a more exaggerated or precise version of the behavior (head turning further to one side, ears moving rapidly, etc.) When you stop reinforcing your dog's first efforts she may get frustrated and try some other things. That's normal. Wait a bit to see if she'll go back to the desired behavior. If your dog seems to be getting more confused, go back and reinforce an easy version of the behavior a few times before trying to raise the criteria again.

8. Some dogs show their confusion and frustration by giving up, laying down and staring at you, or walking away. If this happens it means your dog doesn't understand the game yet, or you're asking for too much too soon. Again, return to reinforcing a very easy, simple version of the behavior.

9. Shaping sessions should be relatively short (5-10 minutes). However, if your dog is enjoying it, work as long as you want. Always end on a good note. Make sure you finish with a successful behavior and reinforcement.

TRICKS

It's really fun to train your dog to do tricks. A snappy finish may impress obedience competitors, but a cute trick is incredibly impressive to friends and family. Throughout this class we work not only on training specific tricks, but on learning how to train any trick. Once your understand the underlying principles, you can train anything the dog is physically capable of doing.

Think about the tricks you would like to train and let me know what they are. We'll work together on formulating techniques to teach these. Even very complicated tricks are possible with a little patience and planning.

WEEK 2 INSTRUCTOR'S GUIDE

1. Have students demonstrate the results of their free shaping over the last week. Address any individual questions or concerns.

2. Talk about increasing demands on the dog (either time or precision). These must be shaped separately. Demonstrate raising criteria with a student's dog. An example: teaching a dog to hold his head on your knee for longer and longer time intervals.

3. Talk about adding and changing cues. Cues should be added after the dog is reliably performing the behavior. Add them at the beginning of the behavior. To change a cue use the new cue first, then the old one. Eventually, the dog will start responding to the new cue.

4. Ask students about the tricks they would like to learn. Take notes.

5. Introduce targeting and talk about elicited (lured) rather than freely emitted behaviors.

Demonstrate how to use the target stick. Have people practice holding the stick, clicker, and treats without their dogs.

Work on conditioning the dog to the target stick. Hold the stick in different positions around the dog. First reinforce glancing at the stick, then sniffing, then moving towards, etc. Accept small behaviors initially. The dog must move towards the stick. Don't touch the stick to your dog's nose. This only teaches the dog to hold still and let you touch him with the stick.

For dogs who absolutely refuse to even glance at the stick you can start by putting a bit of peanut butter or cheese on the stick and reinforce by clicking and allowing the dog to lick the goodie off the stick. However, don't 'bait' the stick more than once or twice.

6. Talk about moveable targets (margarine lid, mat, rug, etc.) Discuss how to start training these.

7. Have students suggest ideas for target tricks. Common ones are crawl, spin, jump, go-out.

8. Tell students that their homework for the coming week is to work on 2 tricks using targets. Tell them not to rush progress, just to show us where they are next week in the training process. The goal is to show a finished behavior at the last class.

9. Talk about using costumes in tricks. Explain desensitization to costumes.

10. Answer any questions and hand out homework sheets.

WEEK 2 HOMEWORK SHEET

INCREASING DEMANDS

As your dog starts to understand and offer a particular behavior, you can increase either the amount of time you require or the precision of the behavior. These increases should occur separately. Do not try to train both at once, you'll just confuse your dog.

For example, you could require your dog to hold his head on your knee for five seconds before you CT. Slowly raise this requirement by several seconds at a time. If your dog ends the behavior before you reinforce, just wait for the behavior to be offered again.

Or, you could increase precision by requiring your dog to put his head on the floor directly between his front paws before you CT. Putting the head on the paws, or on either side of them, does not get reinforced.

In either case, if your dog seems unsure or confused, or quits working, move back to an easier level for a short time. Then quickly increase your requirements again.

ADDING CUES

Once you're getting a behavior fairly regularly you can introduce the signal or cue. At first, use the cue word right before you CT. For example, imagine that your dog is regularly turning her head to the left to earn reinforcement. While your dog is actually doing this quietly say "left", then CT. Over time you can slowly move the word closer to the beginning of the behavior.

Once your dog is performing the behavior every time you use the cue you will stop reinforcing the behavior if it occurs spontaneously. It is at this point that the behavior comes under your control.

If you ever want to change a cue just start using the new one right before the old one. Eventually, your dog will start responding to the new one.

TARGETING

This week we'll move from emitted (spontaneous, freely offered) behaviors, to elicited ones. Elicited behaviors are those that are brought about by some external force. To elicit behaviors we'll using targeting.

A target is any object that your dog is taught to move towards. We'll use both a target stick and a small, moveable target. We will train this behavior by showing the dog the target and CTing for any interest in or movement towards it. Our ultimate goal is to have the dog touch the target with her nose.

Target sticks. A target stick is a handy tool for moving your dog into a number of different positions. It requires a bit of practice to be able to hold the target stick and clicker, and to give treats at the same time. However, it is possible with just a bit of practice. I hold the stick in my right hand across my palm. The clicker is in the same hand between my thumb and index finger. This way I can hold the stick and click with the same hand. I keep treats in my left pocket and use my left hand to deliver treats. Practice the motions without your dog until you can do this easily.

Once you're comfortable using the equipment you can introduce the target stick to your dog. Hold it out and CT your dog for any sign of interest (even a quick shifting of the eyes) towards it. Be ready to CT if your dog looks at the stick or moves towards it. Your target behavior (goal) is to have your dog touch the end of the stick with his nose. You'll need to shape this behavior by first reinforcing any interest, then reinforcing looks, then reinforcing movement towards the stick, then reinforcing any touch, etc. Don't try to rush the process by 'helping' your dog. Hold the stick in different positions around the dog, but do not put the stick on your dog's nose. It's up to your dog to figure out what the requirements for CT are. You don't want to teach your dog to hold still while you touch the stick to his nose.

Once your dog is consistently touching the end of the stick with his nose you can add the 'touch' cue. Then you can encourage your dog to follow the stick as you move it. First, try to get your dog to move one step following the stick, then two, etc. Once your dog is touching and starting to follow the stick we can use it for a number of tricks and behaviors such as jump, crawl, and spin.

Moveable targets. You can choose any small object to use as a moveable target. I like to use a clear margarine lid. Start by showing the target to your dog and CTing for any interest. Follow the steps for conditioning the target stick. Put the target on the floor, and slowly move it further away from you and your dog. Click when your dog goes to the target and treat when she comes back to you. The small target is very useful for teaching the dog to move away from you. This is very useful to teach a dog agility contact zones.

THINGS TO REMEMBER

1. Proceed slowly during the learning stages. Make sure your dog is successful by being very generous with CT at first. Raise your requirements slowly. If your dog seems unsure or confused go back to an easier behavior and CT that for a while. Have faith and patience.

2. Be quiet during training until you start adding the cue. Also, don't move to this stage until your dog is very reliably offering the behavior.

3. Break your training time into lots of short sessions. If you're training more than one behavior you may want to move to a different room or separate the sessions by a short time interval.

4. Don't get boring with your food reinforcers. Variety and surprise lead to better attention and more effort.

5. It's OK for your dog to stop the behavior once he hears the click. Give him the treat and he'll go back to work. A click functions as a release as well as a marker of reinforceable behavior.

WEEK 3 INSTRUCTOR'S GUIDE

1. Have students demonstrate their progress with the target stick and the moveable target. Address questions or problems.

2. Talk about increasing requirements (time or precision) for CT using the targets.

3. Demonstrate some uses of the target stick and moveable target. Encourage students to refine a target trick during the next week.

4. Explain and demonstrate the use of a non-reinforcement marker (NRM) such as 'wrong' or 'oops'.

5. Introduce the retrieve and talk about its uses. Demonstrate and talk about the retrieve as a shaping exercise. Use a non-retriever for your demos!

Brainstorm some ideas for cute retrieve tricks. These might include picking up and carrying a basket, having your dog bring you her leash, and getting the car keys you dropped on the floor.

6. Have students start working on shaping the retrieve. For those who can already retrieve, start working on an unusual object. Homework will be to work on the retrieve this week.

7. Introduce paw tricks such as shake, high 5, and wave. Discuss how to teach these tricks using your hand as a target for your dog's paw. Tell students to work on one paw trick this week.

8. Answer any questions and hand out homework sheets.

WEEK 3 HOMEWORK SHEET

Targeting tricks. Once your dog is consistently touching the stick you can start using it in tricks. An easy trick to start with is a bow. With your dog in a standing position, move the stick between her front feet, slightly in towards her chest. When she moves down and slightly back to touch the stick, CT. You need to be quick to catch the elbows, but not the rest of the dog, on the floor.

Another easy target stick trick is the spin. You simply start slowly moving the stick to one side and CTing as your dog follows it. Work up to a complete circle.

Work on 2 target tricks to show us in the next class.

The non-reinforcement marker (NRM). It's very useful to have a signal to tell the dog that whatever he's doing will not lead to reinforcement. This signal is not a punishment, but a way to inform the dog that a specific action is not productive. You can speed up your training time by using a NRM. Choose a signal such as 'wrong', 'oops', or 'uhn uhn'. Your tone should be neutral, not negative.

The NRM should be conditioned by associating it with the removal of reinforcers. Just as the click means "reinforcement is coming" to your dog, the NRM should mean "reinforcement is not coming".

You can use this signal when your dog is performing a behavior that you didn't ask for. The first few times you do this you may have to use the signal, then gather up your goodies, walk away, and end the training session. Your dog should quickly start to connect this signal with the removal of reinforcement.

RETRIEVE TRICKS

Retrieve tricks can be lots of fun as well as being very useful. You can teach your dog to bring you almost any object with a little patience and practice.

For some dogs retrieving is a very natural behavior, for others it holds no appeal, and some actively resist the idea. The easiest way to teach a retrieve trick is to use shaping to get your dog to approach the object. Start by holding the object and CTing for any interest in it. Then slowly increase your requirements for CT as you did in teaching the target stick. Remember, dogs progress through shaping at very individual rates, so don't try to rush things.

Even if your dog already knows how to retrieve a dumbbell, that doesn't mean he'll hold and retrieve other objects. When starting with a new object, pretend your dog doesn't have any idea what to do and start shaping. This will go very quickly for a dog who already understands the concept of retrieve.

PAW TRICKS

Use your hand as a target to teach paw tricks. If you need to encourage your dog's interest in your hand, hold a treat in your closed fist. When he paws at your hand, click and give him the treat. After your dog starts reliably pawing at your hand keep the treat in your pocket until after the behavior.

Work on one paw trick at a time so that you don't confuse your dog. Make sure one is well-learned before you start working on another. The tricks mostly differ in the position of your hand target: low for the shake, high for the high five, high and moving for the wave.

REMINDER

Next week is our final class. Be prepared to show us your tricks. Don't worry about having a finished product, just show us where you are in the process. You should have several target tricks, a retrieve trick, and a paw trick to share with the class.

WEEK 4 INSTRUCTOR'S GUIDE

1. Have students demonstrate their progress on tricks. Offer comments and suggestions for refining the tricks.

2. Talk about the importance of maintaining attitude and motivation during training by offering a variety of reinforcers. Specifically, discuss non-food reinforcement.

3. Explain the concept of partial reinforcement. Demonstrate how to start applying it using 2fers and 3fers.

4. Introduce the concept of a behavior chain. Show & analyze the parts of a complex behavior such as a retrieve. Discuss back chaining. Brainstorm chaining tricks.

5. Thank everyone for participating. Present options for further training. Give out graduation certificates and doggie bags.

WEEK 4 HOMEWORK SHEET

Thank you for attending this session of Clicks & Tricks. I hope you have enjoyed it as much as I have. I also hope you will continue to use what you have learned in this class to train more tricks. You may also want to use the methods you've learned to teach household manners and obedience exercises. Any behavior can be taught using these principles and ideas.

ALTERNATIVE REINFORCERS

Most trainers rely heavily on food as a primary reinforcer. While there are many good reasons for using food, it's important to use different types of reinforcers as well. Effective reinforcers depend on the individual dog. Some dogs will work hard for praise while others could care less. Some are obsessed with a specific toy and will work for access to it. Many trainers use a quick, exciting game as a reinforcer.

Try to be unpredictable in your use of reinforcers. Have a toy hidden in your pocket and pull it out for a quick game. After a particularly well-performed behavior give your dog an unexpected, large amount of a favorite food reinforcer. Stop in the middle of a training session if your dog has had a breakthrough on a difficult exercise and go for a quick walk. Any object, event, or activity that your dog enjoys can be used as a reinforcer. Observe what your dog does naturally, then control access to that activity and use it as a reinforcer.

PARTIAL REINFORCEMENT

One of our goals in training is to be able to move away from continuously reinforcing behaviors. Continuous reinforcement is necessary whenever the dog is learning something new; it provides the dog with important information about being correct. However, once a behavior is well-learned, we can move to partial reinforcement. Use of partial reinforcement actually encourages the dog to work harder because he never knows when the reinforcer might be coming. Being unpredictable can lead to greater motivation and intensity.

Start moving to partial reinforcement by doing 2fers and 3fers. The dog is required to perform the behavior 2 or 3 times in order to be reinforced. Start by asking your dog to perform a behavior he knows well, give light verbal praise, then release. Then ask for the behavior again and CT. This is a 2fer: 2 behaviors for one reinforcer. Never click without treating, just praise and release for one of the repetitions.

You can also do this with different behaviors, as long as the dog knows them well. For example, ask your dog to sit, praise and release, then ask your dog to down, praise and release, then ask your dog to stand, CT. This is a 3fer.

By using 2fers and 3fers we're slowly getting the dog used to working harder for reinforcement. Don't move to partial reinforcement until your dog is performing the behavior very reliably on cue. When your dog will work well on 2fers and 3fers you can move to even more variable reinforcement. The idea is to keep reinforcement surprising. Sometimes reinforce twice in a row; other times reinforce after 5 behaviors. When your dog can't predict reinforcement, he'll work harder to obtain it.

BEHAVIOR CHAINS

More complicated tricks can be taught by chaining together two or more behaviors. For a behavior chain you need to teach each part separately, then put them together for the finished product. A retrieve is a good example of a behavior chain. It has a number of small components which should be taught individually. Then the parts are put together to be performed on one cue.

Some examples of chained tricks include: picking up toys and putting them in a box, going to and closing a door, opening the refrigerator and getting out a soda, sitting up and begging, etc.

A method called back chaining is often used to put the parts of a chain together. In back chaining you ask the dog to perform the very last behavior in the chain and reinforce that. Then you ask for the next to last behavior, then the last one, then reinforce. You keep working on the chain by adding behaviors to the front, one at a time. Reinforcement always comes after the last behavior. Remember, you've already taught each behavior in the chain before you attempt to put them all together.

Before you begin to train a chained behavior sit down and list each component of the chain. Break it down as far as possible and train each part separately.

***I hope that you will continue to enjoy training your dog using these methods. Dog training is a journey of discovery and creativity. Clicker training can add a whole new dimension to your relationship with your pet. Have fun spending time with your best friend!!

CONCLUSION

Thank you for spending some time learning about teaching your dog tricks and games. Every activity you share with your dog, from taking walks to taking naps to practicing recalls, can help to strengthen the bond between the two of you. Our dogs enjoy being with us and learning new things. If we make it fun and exciting, they like it even more.

Dogs are incredibly bright and intelligent creatures. They are interested in the world around them. They can learn an astounding amount. Keeping them occupied (through constructive activities like tricks and games) serves to keep them out of trouble. A bored, energetic dog tends to cause chaos wherever he goes. But a dog who is focused on his owner and enjoying positive attention is a joy to be around.

I hope that this book has given you some ideas for activities you can share with your best friend. I also hope that it has given you a better understanding of dog behavior and training methods. Learning about dogs and dog training is an ongoing process; you never know it all. It's a journey of continual discovery.

The training methods you use are a reflection of your relationship with your pet. They are an extension of your feelings about your canine companion. Approach your training with love and respect. Be patient, be relaxed, be creative, but most importantly, have fun with your dog.